Treasury of Irish Religious Verse

Treasury of
Irish Religious Verse

EDITED BY
PATRICK MURRAY

With a foreword by
BRENDAN KENNELLY

CROSSROAD · NEW YORK

The Crossroad Publishing Company
370 Lexington Avenue, New York, N.Y. 10017

Printed in England

Library of Congress Cataloging-in-Publication Data

Main entry under title:
Treasury of Irish religious verse.

  Includes indexes.
  1. Religious poetry, English-Irish authors.
2. Religious poetry, Irish. 3. Christian poetry,
English-Irish authors. 4. Religious poetry, Irish-
Translations into English. 5. Religious poetry, English-
Translation from Irish. 6. Ireland-Religion-
Poetry. I. Murray, Patrick, 1935-1984.
II. Kennelly, Brendan.
PR8861.R4T7 1986   821'.008'0382   85-29103
ISBN 0-8245-0776-2

CONTENTS

FOREWORD

Father Patrick Murray has put together an anthology of striking intensity and range. He calls it an anthology of Irish religious verse; and so it is. But it is first and foremost an anthology of valuable poems which will give a great deal of pleasure to readers. Because Father Murray is a man of deep and wide sympathies, he is a probing, adventurous editor. There are no stifling attitudes or paranoid classifications in this book; we have instead an anthology which seeks to explore the religious spirit of man in all its mystery, suffering, terror, exaltation, distraction, doubt, ecstacy and peace, throughout the centuries. This spirit is expressed and explored in poems, some of which reach far back into time while others are the work of contemporary writers. The sense of continuity is startling yet inevitable. What is most striking, to my mind, is not the difference or differences between ancient and modern writers but the similarities, the sense that they experience the same bewilderment and pain, know equal moments of happiness and joy, feel the same doubts and fears, and reach towards similar states of resolution and peace. There *are* differences, of course, but the similarities are more striking. This helps to give the anthology an unusual coherence and concentration.

Father Murray has put a great deal of work and thought into this collection. He has done his research with vigour and wisdom and has produced not only an impressive volume of poems but a panoramic and penetrating view of spiritual life in Ireland for well over a thousand years. It is an epic achievement that leaves us all in this intrepid editor's debt.

Brendan Kennelly

INTRODUCTION

Why an anthology of Irish religious verse? Are there not already available collections of Irish poetry which include such poems? There are indeed such collections, but they cannot do justice to a genre which is so much part of our national heritage and so rich in content as to demand an anthology devoted exclusively to itself. Considering the wealth of material that has accumulated in the course of almost two thousand years — perhaps even more — it is surprising that such an anthology has not appeared long before this. This book is an attempt, however belated, to fill a regrettable literary lacuna.

What identifies a poem as a religious poem? Religion, according to *Chambers Twentieth Century Dictionary*, is 'belief in, recognition of, or an awakening sense of, a higher unseen controlling power or powers, with the emotion and morality connected therewith.' To be religious is to be 'of, connected with, devoted to, or imbued with religion.' As these definitions are wider in connotation than the appellation 'Christian', it is in order to include such poems as *The Mystery*, the first poem in the anthology, which is pantheistic in tone. For the same reason the theosophical poetry of AE is represented.

Ireland's literary history is one of the most ancient in Europe. It begins, according to tradition, with the verse of the legendary Amergin, a Milesian prince or druid and putative author of *The Mystery* and two other strange poems. They are from *The Book of Invasions* — *Leabhar Galbhala* — which is an account of the early semi-mythical conquests of Ireland. In his *Literary History of Ireland* Douglas Hyde claims that these verses 'actually represent the oldest surviving lines in the vernacular of any country in Europe except Greece alone.' However, in *The Story of Early Gaelic Literature* he is more reserved: 'The three short pieces of verse ascribed to Amergin are certainly very ancient and very strange. But as the whole story of the Milesian invasion is wrapped in mystery and is quite possibly a rationalized account of early Irish mythology no faith can be placed in the alleged date or genuineness of Amergin's verses. They are of interest, because as Irish tradition has them as being the first verses made in Ireland, so

9

it may very well be they actually do present the oldest surviving lines of any vernacular tongue in Europe except Greece.'

It would seem that *The Mystery* and its alleged author are destined to remain forever a mystery! I leave the last word on the subject to Aodh de Blacam: 'At whatever time it was composed, it is equally significant to us. It shows us the conception cherished by old Irish writers of the first poet of the race. The poem, as we see, is charged with that natural magic that always is the most fascinating quality of Irish verse; and the legendary Amergin is the prototype of those poets down the ages who, in their poetry, have mixed their souls with Ireland's mountains and waters, her woods, and her tribal hostings on the hilly places' (*Gaelic Literature Surveyed*).

The Voyage of Bran — Immram Bran — is another mysterious poem which gives the impression of belonging to the pagan past. It was composed in the seventh or eighth century and, according to Professor Carney, 'is from beginning to end, a thoroughly Christian poem. It seems, in fact, to be an allegory showing Man setting out on a voyage to Paradise' (*Studies in Irish Literature and History*).

The coming of St Patrick about the middle of the fifth century initiated the most peaceful 'invasion' and the most lasting 'conquest' of all. *The Paschal Fire, The Deer's Cry, The Questions of Ethnu Alba, In Praise of Fionn* record the success of Patrick's mission and the change from paganism to Christianity. Within the next two or three hundred years the hermitage, the monastery and the great schools of learning had become familiar features of the Irish scene. From the eighth to the twelfth century the fine arts flourshed despite the incursions of the Norsemen and the Norman invasion which followed. To this period belong such artistic treasures as the Tara Brooch, the Ardagh Chalice, and such delightful nature poems as *The Hermit's Song, The Scribe, The Lark, God's Praises* etc.

In his introduction to *Ancient Irish Poetry* Kuno Meyer has this to say of Gaelic nature poetry: 'In Nature Poetry the Gaelic muse may vie with that of any other nation. Indeed, these poems occupy a unique position in the literature of the world. To seek out and watch and love Nature, in its tiniest phenomena as in its grandest, was given to no people so early and so fully as to the Celt.'

Many of the later poems recall the dark days of persecution and suppression following the disastrous Battle of Kinsale: the Cromwellian massacres, the confiscation of lands, the Plantations, the Penal Laws, the Famine and the mass emigration that followed. William Drennan has summed it up poignantly in *The Waking of William Orr*:

> Hapless Nation, rent and torn,
> Thou wert early taught to mourn;
> Warfare of six hundred years!
> Epochs marked with blood and tears!

I am reluctant to take issue with so genuine and loyal a friend of Ireland as G. K. Chesterton, but he must surely have let his penchant for the telling couplet run away with his sense of history when he penned the oft quoted lines:

> For the great Gaels of Ireland
> Are the men that God made mad,
> For all their wars are merry,
> And all their songs are sad.

> *(Ballad of the White Horse)*

Wars are never merry — and Irish wars are no exception. Invariably and inevitably war brings in its train death and destruction and suffering, not only for the combatants but for the hapless population of the country or countries involved. And not *all* the songs of the Gael are sad, though many of them are serious. Even in an anthology of religious verse, humour is not excluded: witness *The Merry Jovial Beggar, The Curate's Complaint, Joe's No Saint, An Ulsterman.*

Some readers may question the literary quality or standard of some of the poems chosen for the anthology. That the peasant poet John Keegan's *Irish Reaper's Harvest Hymn* should appear in a volume that also includes the work of poet laureate Cecil Day Lewis may cause some surprise. I call upon another poet, Robert Farren, to be my apologist. In his book *The Course of Irish Verse* he points out that 'John Keegan had the twin advantages of peasant origin and hedge-school teaching: hence the easy natural glances at Faith in *The Irish Reaper's Harvest Hymn* addressed to Our Lady. Of the poets of his time who, as poets could have bought and sold John Keegan, few composed poems more warmly Irish than his, though they wrote *better* poems, absolutely speaking'.

This anthology is directed primarily to the average reader — even to the one who 'has no time for poetry' — rather than to the litterateur. It is hoped that it will be 'popular' in every sense of the word. An anthology is of necessity the choice of an individual. Consequently, readers may be disappointed to find that their favourite poem or poems or poet have been omitted. This is inevitable. However, it is hoped that everyone may find some poem that is pleasing and that raises the mind to him who is the Beginning and the End and the loving Father of all.

Commentary on our contemporary poets or on their immediate predecessors is unnecessary and would unduly extend this Introduction. I shall let them speak for themselves, or rather, allow their poems to speak for them. In many instances these reveal an attitude to spiritual values and beliefs unsuspected by those acquainted only with their more popular poems. The veil is momentarily drawn aside and we glimpse the creature before his God, the child before his Father. This perhaps is an example of that divine discontent so eloquently expressed by Francis Thompson in *The Hound of Heaven:*

> Ah, fondest, blindest, weakest,
> I am He whom thou seekest!
> Thou dravest love from thee who dravest me.

and expressed too by Saint Augustine in his *Confessions:*

> Thou hast made us for Thyself, O Lord,
> Our hearts are restless until they rest in Thee.

Before concluding the Introduction I wish to express my sincere gratitude to all who in any way helped in the production of this anthology. I am indebted first of all and most of all to Professor Brendan Kennelly of Trinity College, Dublin, to whom I submitted the manuscript in its early stages for his expert opinion. His own anthology, *The Penguin Book of Irish Verse*, is already a classic. His positive and encouraging response was the stimulus which decided me to persevere with the work. For this and for his generous and valuable contribution to the contents of the anthology I am most grateful.

To the Right Reverend Dr G. O. Simms I am indebted for the poems of Helen Waddell, Richard Chenevix Trench, Stephen L. Gwynne and George Seaver. I thank him for his kind encouragement and for his co-operation.

I am grateful also to the many poets who responded so generously to my request for permission to include their poems. A special word of thanks to Fr Raymond Murray and Dr Máirtín O Direan who translated their poems from Irish for the anthology.

I am also deeply grateful to Seamus Heaney for his excerpt from his moving translation of the spiritual classic of St John of the Cross which he is preparing for publication. His generosity is sincerely appreciated. It is interesting to note that between his poem, the most recent in the anthology, and Amergin's *The Mystery*, possibly the first poem composed in Ireland, there is a time span of what could be more than two thousand years!

I wish to thank Dr Muriel McCarthy of Marsh's Library, Miss Paula Howard of the Gilbert Library, Mr Maurice Curtis of the Central Catholic Library, the Librarian and staff of the National Library, the Royal Irish Academy Librarian, the RDS Library, and Rathmines Public Library. To all of them I am grateful for their courtesy and co-operation.

Last but by no means least, to Charlotte Westbrook, designer of the book, and to Michael Adams my sincere gratitude for their patience, courtesy and co-operation.

AMERGIN

Translation by Douglas Hyde

A Milesian prince, brother of Evir, Ir and Eremon said to have colonised Ireland hundreds of years before Christ. According to tradition these verses are the first to have been composed in Ireland. They are ascribed to Amergin and are from the Leabhar Gabhala, or Book of Invasions.

The Mystery

I am the wind which breathes upon the sea,
I am the wave of the ocean,
I am the murmur of the billows,
I am the ox of the seven combats,
I am the vulture upon the rocks,
I am a beam of the sun,
I am the fairest of plants,
I am the wild boar in valour,
I am a salmon in the water,
I am a lake in the plain,
I am a word of science,
I am the point of the lance of battle,
I am the God who created in the head the fire.
Who is it who throws light into the meeting on the mountain?
Who announces the ages of the moon?
Who teaches the place where couches the sun?

(If not I)

ANONYMOUS

(5th century)

Translation by Eleanor Hull

The Song of Childbirth

O Ness, let all men stand,
The hour of thy peril is at hand;
Pale daughter of old Eochad, Buidhe the mild
We rise to greet thy child!
Wife of the ruddy palms
Let not the mind be filled with terror's qualms;
The head of hosts, the one
Whom thousands shall extol, shall be thy son.

In the same timely hour upon this earth
He and the King of the World have their birth;
Through the long ages' gloom
Now and to the day of doom
Praises shall echo through the realm of life.
Heroes, at sight of him, cease their strife;
Hostages they twain shall never be
The Christ and he.

On the plain of Inisfail he shall come forth,
On the flag-stone of the meadow to the North.
Hostages every battle-chief to him will send,
Through the great world his glory will extend;
The king of grace is he,
The Hound of Ulster he;
But and if he falls,
Darkness and woe descend on Erin's halls.

Conchobhar, son of Ness 'ungentle', is his name;
Raids and red routs his valour will proclaim.
There he will find his death

King Conchobhar was believed to be born in the same year as Jesus Christ, and to have met his death in endeavouring to avenge the death of Christ.

Where the expiring breath
of the suffering God his vengeful sword demands,
In the dark hour upon the Holy Lands;
Shining his red sword's track,
Over the sloping plain of Liam's back.

ANONYMOUS
(7th century)

Translation by James Carney

The Questions of Ethne Alba

Who is God
and where is God,
of whom is God,
and where His dwelling?

Has He sons and daughters,
gold and silver, this God of yours?

Is He ever-living?
is He beautiful,
was His Son
fostered by many?

Are His daughters
dear and beautiful
to the men of the world?

Is He in heaven
or on the earth?
In the sea,
in the rivers,
in the mountains,
in the valleys?

Speak to us
tidings of Him:
How will He be seen,
how is He loved,
how is He found?

Is it in youth
or is it in old age
He is found?

Attributed to ST PATRICK
(8th century)

Translation by Kuno Meyer

Saint Patrick's Breastplate or The Deer's Cry

I arise today
Through a mighty strength, the invocation of the Trinity,
Through belief in the threeness,
Through confession of the oneness
Of the Creator of Creation.

I arise today
Through the strength of Christ's birth with His baptism,
Through the strength of His crucifixion with His burial,
Through the strength of His resurrection with His ascension,
Through the strength of His descent for the judgment of Doom.

I arise today
Through the strength of the love of Cherubim,
In obedience of angels,
In the service of archangels,
In hope of resurrection to meet with reward,
In prayers of patriarchs,
In predictions of prophets,
In preaching of apostles,
In faiths of confessors,
In innocence of holy virgins,
In deeds of righteous men.

I arise today
Through the strength of heaven:
Light of sun,
Radiance of moon,
Splendour of fire,
Speed of lightning,
Swiftness of wind,
Depth of sea,
Stability of earth,
Firmness of rock.

I arise today
Through God's strength to pilot me:
God's might to uphold me,
God's wisdom to guide me,
God's eye to look before me,
God's ear to hear me,
God's word to speak for me,
God's hand to guard me,
God's way to lie before me,
God's shield to protect me,
God's host to save me
From snares of devils,
From temptation of vices,
From every one who shall wish me ill,
Afar and anear,
Alone and in a multitude.

I summon today all these powers between me and those evils,
Against every cruel merciless power that may oppose my body and
       soul,
Against incantations of false prophets,
Against black laws of pagandom,
Against false laws of heretics,
Against craft of idolatry,
Against spells of women and smiths and wizards,
Against every knowledge that corrupts man's body and soul.

Christ to shield me today
Against poison, against burning,
Against drowning, against wounding,
So that there may come to me abundance of reward.
Christ with me, Christ before me, Christ behind me,
Christ in me, Christ beneath me, Christ above me,
Christ on my right, Christ on my left,
Christ when I lie down, Christ when I sit down, Christ when I
      arise,
Christ in the heart of every man who thinks of me,
Christ in the mouth of every one who speaks of me,
Christ in every eye that sees me,
Christ in every ear that hears me.

I arise today
Through a mighty strength, the invocation of the Trinity,
Through belief in the threeness,
Through confession of the oneness
Of the Creator of Creation.

ANONYMOUS
(8th century)

Translation by Frank O'Connor

Suibhne (Sweeney) the King, flying from the battlefield, is driven mad by the sight of the broken bodies. From a twelfth-century romance based on eighth century material.

The Sweetness of Nature

Endlessly over the water
    Birds of the Bann are singing;
Sweeter to me their voices
    Than any churchbell's ringing.

Over the plain of Moyra
    Under the heels of foemen
I saw my people broken
    As flax is scutched by women.

But the cries I hear by Derry
    Are not of men triumphant;
I hear their calls in the evening,
    Swans calm and exultant.

I hear the stag's belling
    Over the valley's steepness;
No music on the earth
    Can move me like its sweetness.

Christ, Christ hear me!
    Christ, Christ of thy meekness!
Christ, Christ love me!
    Sever me not from thy sweetness!

ANONYMOUS
(8th century)

Translation by Frank O'Connor

Oisin, son of Fionn, having spent many years in Tir na n'Og because of his love of a fairy queen, returns to Ireland to find Fionn and his warriors dead and St Patrick and his monks in control. The poem reflects the spirit of the Ossianic verse of the eighth and ninth centuries, though it is probably much later.

The Praise of Fionn

Patrick, you chatter too loud
　　And lift your crozier too high,
Your stick would be kindling soon
　　If my son Osgar stood by.

If my son Osgar and God
　　Wrestled it out on the hill
And I saw Osgar go down
　　I'd say that your God fought well.

But how could the God you praise
　　And his mild priests singing a tune
Be better than Fionn the swordsman,
　　Generous, faultless Fionn?

Just by the strength of their hands
　　The Fenians' battles were fought,
With never a spoken lie,
　　Never a lie in thought.

There never sat priest in church
　　A tuneful psalm to raise
Better spoken than these
　　Scarred in a thousand frays.

Whatever your monks have called
　　The law of the King of Grace,
That was the Fenians' Law;
　　His home is their dwelling-place.

If happier house than Heaven
    There be, above or below,
'Tis there my master Fionn
    And his fighting men will go.

Ah, priest, if you saw the Fenians
    Filling the strand beneath
Or gathered in streamy Naas
    You would praise them with every breath.

Patrick, ask of your God
    Does he remember their might,
Or has he seen east or west
    Better men in a fight?

Or known in his own land
    Above the stars and the moon
For wisdom, courage and strength
    A man the like of Fionn?

ANONYMOUS
(8th century)

Translation by Kuno Meyer

The Song of the Woman
From *The Voyage of Bran*

One day, in the neighbourhood of his stronghold, Bran went about alone, when he heard music behind him. As often as he looked back, 'twas still behind him the music was. At last he fell asleep at the music, such was its sweetness. When he awoke from his sleep, he saw close by him a branch of silver with white blossoms, nor was it easy to distinguish its bloom from that branch. Then Bran took the branch in his hand to his royal house. When the hosts were in the royal house, they saw a woman in strange raiment on the floor of the house. 'Twas then she sang the fifty quatrains to Bran, while the host heard her, and all beheld the woman.

'A great birth will come after ages,
That will not be in a lofty place,
The son of a woman whose mate will not be known,
He will seize the rule of the many thousands.

'A rule without beginning, without end,
He has created the world so that it is perfect,
Whose are earth and sea,
Woe to him that shall be under His unwill!

"Tis He that made the heavens,
Happy he that has a white heart,
He will purify hosts under pure water,
'Tis He will heal your sicknesses . . .

'It is a law of pride in this world
To believe in the creatures, to forget God,
Overthrow by diseases, and old age,
Destruction of the soul through deception.

'A noble salvation will come
From the King who has created us,
A white law will come over seas,
Besides being God, He will be man.'

The Worship of Cromm Cruaich
From The Voyage of Bran

Here used to be
A high idol with many fights,
Which was named the Cromm Cruaich:
It made every tribe to be without peace.

'Twas a sad evil!
Brave Gaels used to worship it.
From it they would not without tribute ask
To be satisfied as to their portion of the hard world.

He was their god,
The withered Cromm with many mists,
The people whom he shook over every host,
The everlasting kingdom they shall not have.

To him without glory
They would kill their piteous wretched offspring
With much wailing and peril,
To pour their blood around Cromm Cruaich.

Milk and corn
They would ask from him speedily
In return for one third of their healthy issue:
Great was the horror and the scare of him.

To him
Noble Gaels would prostrate themselves,
From the worship of him, with many manslaughters,
The plain is called Mag Slecht.

Around Cromm Cruaich
There the hosts would prostrate themselves.
Though he put them under deadly disgrace,
Their name clings to the noble plain.

In their ranks (stood)
Four times three stone idols.
To bitterly beguile the hosts
The figure of the Cromm was made of gold.

Since the rule
Of Herimon, the noble man of grace,
There was worshipping of stones
Until the coming of good Patrick of Macha.

A sledge hammer to the Cromm
He applied from crown to sole,
He destroyed without lack of valour
The feeble idol which was here.

ANONYMOUS

(8th century)

Translation by Eugene O'Curry

Litany to Our Lady

O Great Mary.

O Mary, greatest of Maries.

O Greatest of Women.

O Queen of Angels.

O Mistress of the Heavens.

O Woman full and replete with the grace of the Holy Ghost.

O Blessed and Most Blessed.

O Mother of Eternal Glory.

O Mother of the heavenly and earthly Church.

O Mother of Love and Indulgence.

O Mother of the Golden Heights.

O Honour of the Sky.

O Sign of Tranquillity.

O Gate of Heaven.

O Golden Casket.

O Couch of Love and Mercy.

O Temple of Divinity.

O Beauty of Virgins.

O Mistress of the Tribes.

O Fountain of the Parterres.

O Cleansing of the Sins.

O Purifying of Souls.

O Mother of Orphans.

O Breast of the Infants.

O Solace of the Wretched.

O Star of the Sea.

O Handmaid of the Lord.

O Mother of Christ.

O Resort of the Lord.

O Graceful like the Dove.

O Serene like the Moon.

O Resplendent like the Sun.

O Cancelling Eve's disgrace.

O Regeneration of Life.
O Beauty of Women.
O Leader of the Virgins.
O Enclosed Garden.
O Closely Locked Fountain.
O Mother of God.
O Perpetual Virgin.
O Holy Virgin.
O Serene Virgin.
O Chaste Virgin.
O Temple of the Living God.
O Royal Throne of the Eternal King.
O Sanctuary of the Holy Ghost.
O Virgin of the Root of Jesse.
O Cedar of Mount Lebanon.
O Cypress of Mount Sion.
O Crimson Rose of the Land of Jacob.
O Blooming like the Palm Tree.
O Fruitful like the Olive Tree.
O Glorious Son-Bearer.
O Light of Nazareth.
O Glory of Jerusalem.
O Beauty of the World.
O Noblest-Born of the Christian Flock.
O Queen of Life.
O Ladder of Heaven.

ANONYMOUS
(8th century)

Translation by Brendan Kennelly

God's Praises

Only a fool would fail
To praise God in His might
When the tiny mindless birds
Praise Him in their flight.

Christ's Bounty

I pray you, Christ, to change my heart,
    To make it whole;
Once you took on flesh like mine,
    Now take my soul.

Ignominy and pain you knew,
    The lash, the scourge,
You, the perfect molten metal
    Of my darkened forge.

You make the bright sun bless my head,
    Put ice beneath my feet,
Send salmon swarming in the tides,
    Give crops of wheat.

When Eve's wild children come to you
    With prayerful words,
You crowd the rivers with fine fish,
    The sky with birds.

You make the small flowers thrive
    In the wholesome air,
You spread sweetness through the world.
    What miracle can compare?

Saint, Bird, Angel

Saint Anfaidh walked alone
    Where a thin stream was flowing
And there he saw a little bird
    Sorrowing.

'God', he thought, 'What's happening?
    I cannot think;
But till I understand, I shall not
    Eat or drink.'

An angel stood beside him,
    And quietly said,
'Mo Lua, gentle son of Ocha,
    Has just died.

'All living things lament him,
    He was loved by all,
He never killed a living thing
    Great or small.

'The beast laments him with his cry
    Man with a tender word,
And look, beside you, grieving stands
    A little bird.'

Jesus on the Sabbath

Jesus, son of the living God,
    Was five years old; one day
He blessed twelve small pools
    And fenced them in with clay.

Twelve little birds he shaped,
    Passeres they are called;
He made them on the Sabbath
    Of clay without a fault.

A certain Jew attacked him,
    Son of the living God,
And to his father Joseph
    He led him by the hand.

'Keep an eye on your son, Joseph,
    How badly he behaves!
Imagine! On the Sabbath
    He makes images of birds.'

Jesus clapped his hands,
   His young voice they heard
And then before their eyes
   He scattered the little birds.

He said, 'That you may know who made you
   Return to your homes to-night;'
Then someone shouted that he heard
   The cries of birds in flight.

ANONYMOUS
(8th-10th century)

Translation by Robin Flower

The Good Man
This is the song the Devil sang to Saint Moling.

Pure gold, bright sky about the sun,
A silver goblet filled with wine,
An angel wise is everyone
That still hath done God's will divine.

A caught bird fluttering in the snare,
A leaky ship that wild winds shake,
A wineglass drained, a rotten tree —
Even such they be that God's law break.

A breathing branch that flowers in spring,
A vessel brimmed with honey sweet,
A precious ruby beyond price —
Such he that follows Christ's own feet.

A hollow nut that none desire,
A savour foul, a rotten wood,
A flowerless crabtree growing wild,
Are those defiled that Christ withstood.

The man that does Christ's heavenly will,
He is the sun that warms the year,
God's image through his heart doth pass,
He is a glass of crystal clear.

A racehorse straining for the goal,
Heaven is the mark for which he tries;
That chariot driven by a king,
A precious thing shall be his prize.

A sun that warms all Heaven round,
God loves him more than things of price:
A noble temple and divine,
A golden shrine of sacrifice.

An altar with the wine outpoured
Where sweet choirs sing in linen stoled,
A chalice with God's blood therein
Of findruine or precious gold.

The Scribe

Over my head the woodland wall
Rises; the ousel sings to me.
Above my booklet lined for words
The woodland birds shake out their glee.

There's the blithe cuckoo chanting clear
In mantle grey from bough to bough!
God keep me still! for here I write
A scripture bright in great woods now.

The White Lake

When holy Patrick full of grace
Suffered on Cruach, that blest place,
In grief and gloom enduring then
For Eire's women, Eire's men,

God for his comfort sent a flight
Of birds angelically bright
That sang above the darkling lake
A song unceasing for his sake.

'Twas thus they chanted, all and some,
'Come hither, Patrick! hither come!
Shield of the Gael, thou light of story,
Appointed star of golden glory!'

Thus singing all those fair birds smite
The waters with soft wings in flight
Till the dark lake its gloom surrenders
And rolls a tide of silvery splendours.

The Lark

Learned in music sings the lark,
I leave my cell to listen;
His open beak spills music, hark!
Where Heaven's bright cloudlets glisten.

And so I'll sing my morning psalm
That God bright Heaven may give me
And keep me in eternal calm
And from all sin relieve me.

ALCUIN
(c. 735-804)

Translation by Helen Waddell

A Sequence for Saint Michael
which Alcuin wrote for the Emperor Charles

Michael, Archangel of the King of Kings,
Give ear to our voices.

We acknowledge thee to be the Prince of the citizens of heaven:
And at thy prayer God sends His angels unto men,

That the enemy with cunning craft shall not prevail
To do the hurt he craves to weary men.
Yea, thou hast the dominion of perpetual Paradise,
And ever do the holy angels honour thee.

Thou wert seen in the Temple of God,
A censer of gold in thy hands,
And the smoke of it fragrant with spices
Rose up till it came before God.

Thou with strong hand didst smite the cruel dragon,
And many souls didst rescue from his jaws.
Then was there a great silence in heaven,
And a thousand thousand saying 'Glory to the Lord King.'

Hear us, Michael, greatest angel,
Come down a little from thy seat,
To bring us the strength of God,
And the lightening of His mercy.

And do thou, Gabriel,
Lay low our foes,
And thou, Raphael,
Heal our sick,
Purge our disease, ease thou our pain,
And give us to share
In the joys of the blessed.

Emperor, thy scholar made these verses for thee.

Jesukin

Jesukin
Lives my little cell within;
What were wealth of cleric high —
All is lie but Jesukin.

Nursling nurtured, as 'tis right,
Harbours here no servile spright,
Jesu, of the skies, who art
Next my heart through every night.

Jesukin, my good for aye,
Calling and will not have nay,
King of all things, ever true,
He shall have me who will away.

Jesu, more than angel aid,
Fosterling not formed to fade,
Nursed by me in desert wild,
Jesu, Child of Judah's Maid.

Sons of kings and kingly kin
To my land may enter in;
Guest of none I hope to be
Save of Thee, my Jesukin.

Unto heaven's High King confest
Sing a chorus, maidens blest!
He is o'er us, though within
Jesukin is on our breast.

ANONYMOUS

(9th century)

Translation by Kuno Meyer

The Hermit's Song

I wish, O Son of the living God,
O ancient, eternal King,
For a hidden little hut in the wilderness
That it may be my dwelling.

An all-grey lithe little lark
To be by its side,
A clear pool to wash away sins
Through the grace of the Holy Spirit.

Quite near, a beautiful wood,
Around it on every side,
To nurse many-voiced birds,
Hiding it with its shelter.

And facing the south for warmth;
A little brook across its floor,
A choice land with many gracious gifts
Such as be good for every plant.

A few men of sense —
We will tell their number —
Humble and obedient,
To pray to the King:

Four times three, three times four,
Fit for every need,
Twice six in the church,
Both north and south:

Six pairs besides myself,
Praying forever to the King
Who makes the sun shine.

A pleasant church and with the linen altar-cloth,
A dwelling for God from Heaven;
Then, shining candles
Above the pure white Scriptures.

One house for all to go to
For the care of the body,
Without ribaldry, without boasting,
Without thought of evil.

This is the husbandry I would take,
I would choose, and will not hide it:
Fragrant leek,
Hens, salmon, trout, bees.

Raiment and food enough for me
From the King of fair fame,
And I to be sitting for a while
Praying God in every place.

ANONYMOUS
(9th century)

Translation by Eleanor Hull

A Prayer

Be thou my vision, O Lord of my heart,
Naught is all else to me, save that Thou art.

Thou my best thought by day and by night,
Waking or sleeping, Thy presence my light.

Be Thou my wisdom, Thou my true word;
I ever with Thee, Thou with me, Lord.

Thou my great father, I Thy dear son;
Thou in me dwelling, I with Thee one.

Be Thou my battle-shield, sword for the fight,
Be Thou my dignity, Thou my delight.

Thou my soul's shelter, Thou my high tower;
Raise Thou me heavenward, power of my power.

Riches I heed not, nor man's empty praise,
Thou mine inheritance now and always.

Thou, and Thou only, first in my heart,
High King of heaven, my treasure Thou art.

King of the seven heavens, grant me for dole,
Thy love in my heart, Thy light in my soul.

Thy light from my soul, Thy love from my heart,
King of the seven heavens, may they never depart.

With the high king of heaven, after victory won,
May I reach heaven's joys, O bright heaven's sun!

Heart of my own heart, whatever befall,
Still be my vision, O Ruler of all.

I lie down with God

I lie down with God, and may God lie down with me;
The right hand of God under my head,
The two hands of Mary round about me,
The cross of the nine white angels
From the back of my head
To the sole of my feet.
May I not lie with evil,
And may evil not lie with me.

ANONYMOUS
(10th century)

Translation by Brendan Kennelly

On the Flightiness of Thought

Shame to all my thoughts now
    How they skip and stray,
This will be my danger
    On the Judgment day.

At the singing of the psalms
    My thoughts take another road,
Giddy, fretful, always
    Forgetting about God.

With wanton women
    Beckoning in the mind
Through woods, through cities — swifter
    Than any wind

Now in a sweet meadow
    Now in a place of shame
Now in a banquet-hall
    In a country without a name.

Unhelped by even the slightest craft
    They make light of every sea;
One leap from earth to heaven
    Proves their agility.

They run the race of folly
    Far and near;
After a daft spin through time and space
    They come back here

And if I shackled their hands, fettered their feet,
    Tethered them to my own breast,
Do you think that would stop them?
    They'd never rest.

Sword and whip are helpless
        To keep them down,
Eels bellying through grasses
        Of the mind's moist ground.

No lock of jail or dungeon
        Can hold them back,
No man-made chains will keep them
        From their crazy track.

O Christ
        To you such things are clear
Help me to net these thoughts
        To keep them here

Locked in my mind's cold cell,
        Feeling the chill
Discipline that makes me hope
        I do your will.

Attributed to ST COLUM CHILLE (d.597)

(10th century)

Translation by Kuno Meyer and John Strachan

Prayer to the Virgin

Gentle Mary, noble maiden, give us help!
Shrine of our Lord's body, casket of the mysteries!

Queen of queens, pure holy maiden,
Pray for us that our wretched transgression be forgiven for thy sake.

Merciful one, forgiving one, with the grace of the Holy Spirit,
Pray with us to the true-judging King of the goodly ambrosial clan.

Branch of Jesse's tree in the beauteous hazel-wood,
Pray for me until I obtain forgiveness of my foul sins.

Mary, splendid diadem, thou that hast saved our race,
Glorious torch, orchard of Kings!

Brilliant one, transplendent one, with the deed of pure chastity,
Fair golden illumined ark, holy daughter from Heaven!

Mother of righteousness, Thou that excellest all else,
Pray with me thy first-born to save me on the day of Doom.

Noble rare star, tree under blossom,
Powerful choice lamp, sun that warmeth every one.

Ladder of the great track by which every saint ascends,
Mayest thou be our safeguard towards the glorious Kingdom.

Fair fragrant seat chosen by the King,
The noble guest who was in thy womb three times three months.

Glorious royal porch through which He was incarnated,
The splendid chosen sun, Jesus, Son of the living God.

For the sake of the fair babe that was conceived in thy womb,
For the sake of the holy child that is High-King in every place,

For the sake of His cross that is higher than any cross,
For the sake of His burial when He was buried in the stone tomb,

For the sake of His resurrection when He arose before everyone,
For the sake of the holy household from every place to Doom,

Be thou our safeguard in the Kingdom of the good Lord,
That we may meet with dear Jesus — that is our prayer — hail!

AENGUS THE CULDEE
(10th century)

Translation by Eoin Neeson

A Prayer for Forgiveness

Forgive, O Lord, this worldly one
For I repent the sins I've done:
Forgive me all that You may see,
Dear gentle Christ, of Your mercy.

For Your loved humanity
For Your blessed nativity,
For Your purging of the world,
Forgive, O King, the sins I've hurled.

For Your devoted crucifixion,
For Your glorious resurrection,
For my passions grant me pardon,
Merciful and sacred Lord.

May Your Ascension into heaven
To Your Father, dear Lord, lessen
All the evils I have made
As, dear Christ, You truly said.

When You come to judge the world
For which we have God's very word,
Before God's hosts I humbly pray,
Wash my naked sins away.

For every holy maiden here,
For every man who holds you dear,
For wonder of the Virgin Mother
Forgive my sins, beloved Father.

ANONYMOUS

(11th century)

Translation by Eleanor Hull

The Soul's Desire

It were my soul's desire
To see the face of God;
It were my soul's desire
To rest in His abode.

It were my soul's desire
To study zealously;
This, too, my soul's desire,
A clear rule set for me.

It were my soul's desire
A spirit free from gloom;
It were my soul's desire
New life beyond the Doom.

It were my soul's desire
To shun the chills of Hell;
Yet more my soul's desire
Within His house to dwell.

It were my soul's desire
To imitate my King,
It were my soul's desire
His ceaseless praise to sing.

It were my soul's desire
When heaven's gate is won
To find my soul's desire
Clear shining like the sun.

Grant, Lord, my soul's desire,
Deep waves of cleansing sighs;
Grant, Lord, my soul's desire
From earthly cares to rise.

This still my soul's desire
Whatever life afford —
To gain my soul's desire
And see Thy face, O Lord.

ANONYMOUS
(Date unknown)

Translation by Kuno Meyer

The Crucifixion

At the cry of the first bird
They began to crucify Thee, O cheek like a swan,
It were not right ever to cease lamenting —
It was like the parting of day from night.

Ah! though sore the suffering
Put upon the body of Mary's Son —
Sorer to Him was the grief
That was put upon her for His sake.

FLANN FIONN

(12th century)

Translation by James Clarence Mangan

In his Life of Saint Cuthbert *the Venerable Bede refers to Prince Alfrid's presence as a student in Ireland about the year 684.*

Alfrid's Itinerary through Ireland

I found in Innisfail the fair,
In Ireland, while in exile there,
Women of worth, both grave and gay men,
Many clerics and many laymen.

I travelled its fruitful provinces round,
And in every one of the five I found,
Alike in church and in palace hall,
Abundant apparel, and food for all.

Gold and silver I found, and money,
Plenty of wheat and plenty of honey;
I found God's people rich in pity,
Found many a feast and many a city.

I also found in Armagh, the splendid,
Meekness, wisdom, and prudence blended,
Fasting, as Christ hath recommended,
And noble councillors untranscended.

I found in each great church moreo'er,
Whether on island or on shore,
Piety, learning, fond affection
Holy welcome and kind protection.

I found the good lay monks and brothers
Ever beseeching help for others,
And in their keeping the holy word
Pure as it came from Jesus the Lord.

I found in Munster unfettered of any,
Kings, and queens, and poets a many —
Poets well skilled in music and measure,
Prosperous doings, mirth and pleasure.

I found in Connaught the just, redundance
Of riches, milk in lavish abundance;
Hospitality, vigor, fame,
In Cruachan's land of heroic name.

I found in the county of Connall the glorious,
Bravest heroes, ever victorious;
Fair-complexioned men and warlike,
Ireland's lights, the high, the starlike!

I found in Ulster, from hill to glen,
Hardy warriors, resolute men,
Beauty that bloomed when youth was gone,
And strength transmitted from sire to son.

I found in Leinster the smooth and sleek,
From Dublin to Slewmargy's peak;
Flourishing pastures, valour, health,
Long-living worthies, commerce, wealth.

I found, besides, from Ara to Glea,
In the broad rich country of Ossorie,
Sweet fruits, good laws for all and each,
Great chess-players, men of truthful speech.

I found in Meath's fair principality,
Virtue, vigor, and hospitality;
Candor, joyfulness, bravery, purity,
Ireland's bulwark and security.

I found strict morals in age and youth,
I found historians recording truth;
The things I sing of in verse unsmooth,
I found them all — I have written sooth.

ANONYMOUS
(13th century)

Translation by Kuno Meyer

Hospitality in Ancient Ireland

Oh King of stars!
Whether my house be dark or bright,
Never shall it be closed against any one,
Lest Christ close His house against me.

If there be a guest in your house
And you conceal aught from him,
'Tis not the guest that will be without it,
But Jesus, Mary's Son.

DONNCHADH MOR O DALA
(Died 1244)

Translation by Sean O'Faolain

At Saint Patrick's Purgatory

Pity me on my pilgrimage to Loch Derg!
O King of the churches and the bells —
bewailing your sores and your wounds,
but not a tear can I squeeze from my eyes!

Not moisten an eye
after so much sin!
Pity me, O King! What shall I do
with a heart that seeks only its own ease?

Without sorrow or softening in my heart,
bewailing my faults without repenting them!
Patrick the high priest never thought
that he would reach God in this way.

O lone son of Calpurn — since I name him —
O Virgin Mary, how sad is my lot! —
he was never seen as long as he was in this life
without the track of tears from his eyes.

In a narrow, hard, stone-wall cell
I lie after all my sinful pride —
O woe, why cannot I weep a tear! —
and I buried alive in the grave.

On the day of Doom we shall weep heavily,
both clergy and laity;
the tear that is not dropped in time,
none heeds in the world beyond.

I shall have you go naked, go unfed,
body of mine, father of sin,
for if you are turned Hellwards
little shall I reck your agony tonight.

O only begotten Son by whom all men were made,
who shunned not the death by three wounds,
pity me on my pilgrimage to Lough Derg
and I with a heart not softer than a stone!

Fair is Our Lord's Own City

Translation from the Irish by Coslett Quin

O fair is our Lord's own city,
With clearest light abloom
And full of joy and music,
Where woe can never come.

No guilt or condemnation
Its citizens may know,
None weary is, none anxious,
Nor head by grief bent low.

The holy gracious Spirit
Shines there with brightest beams,
And sheds God's royal bounty
In shining showers and streams.

The saints and martyrs countless,
Who in this world found woe,
Find there a peace and pleasure
The world cannot bestow.

From earth our faces turning
Towards the King of grace;
In prayer let us beseech him
To bring us to that place.

THOMAS DE CELANO

(13th century)

Translation from the Latin by Wentworth Dillon

The Day of Judgment

The day of Wrath, that dreadful day,
Shall the whole world in ashes lay,
As David and the Sibyls say.

What horror will invade the mind,
When the strict Judge, who would be kind,
Shall have few venial faults to find.

The last loud trumpet's wondrous sound
Shall through the rending tombs rebound,
And wake the nations underground.

Nature and death shall with surprise
Behold the pale offender rise,
And view the Judge with conscious eyes.

Then shall, with universal dread,
The sacred mystic book be read,
To try the living and the dead.

The Judge ascends his awful throne,
He makes each secret sin be known,
And all with shame confess their own.

Oh then, what interest shall I make,
To save my last important stake,
When the most just have cause to quake?

Thou mighty, formidable King,
Thou Mercy's unexhausted spring,
Some comfortable pity bring!

Forget not what my ransom cost,
Nor let my dear-bought soul be lost,
In storms of guilty terror tost.

Thou, who for me didst feel such pain,
Whose precious blood the cross did stain,
Let not these agonies be vain.

Thou whom avenging powers obey,
Cancel my debt (too great to pay)
Before the sad accounting day.

Surrounded with amazing fears,
Whose load my soul with anguish bears,
I sigh, I weep; accept my tears.

Thou, who wert moved by Mary's grief,
And, by absolving of the thief,
Hast given me hope, now give relief.

Reject not my unworthy prayer,
Preserve me from that dangerous snare,
Which Death and gaping Hell prepare.

Give my exalted soul a place
Among the chosen right-hand race,
The sons of God and heirs of Grace.

From that insatiable abyss
Where flames devour and serpents hiss,
Promote me to thy seat of bliss.

Prostrate my contrite heart I rend,
My God, my Father, and my Friend,
Do not forsake me in my end.

Well may they curse their second breath,
Who rise to a revived death;
Thou great Creator of mankind.
Let guilty man compassion find.

RICHARD DE LEDREDE
(14th century)

Translation from the Latin by Robert Wyse Jackson

The Festival of the Nativity

Bestow this day on us the grace
    Upon this solemn Festival to see
    The wonder of Our Lord's Nativity.

Bestow this day on us the grace
    To order so our way of life within
    That it is free from grief or stain of sin.

Bestow this day on us the grace
    To mend our ways through life's successive hours
    And gather, as a garland, goodness' flowers.

Bestow this day on us the grace
    So blithely in the joy of God to live
    That those who hurt us, we this day forgive.

Bestow this day on us the grace
    To carol for the Birthday of our King
    And, as a gift, an honest heart to bring.

Bestow, bestow this day on us
    For healing of our griefs, His Merit's Strength,
    And bear us joyful to His Throne at length.

SAINT JOHN OF THE CROSS
(1542-1591)

Translation by Seamus Heaney

Song of the Soul that knows God by Faith

How well I know that fountain,
filling, running,
    although it is the night.

That eternal fountain hidden away,
I know its haven and its secrecy
    although it is the night.

But not its source because it does not have one
which is all sources' source and origin
    although it is the night.

No other thing can be so beautiful.
Here the earth and heaven drink their fill
    although it is the night.

I know no sounding-line can find its bottom,
nobody ford or plumb its deepest fathom
    although it is the night.

And its current so in flood it overspills
to water hell and heaven and all peoples
    although it is the night.

And the current that is generated there,
as far as it wills, it can flow that far
    although it is the night.

And from these two a third current proceeds
which neither of these two, I know, precedes
    although it is the night.

This eternal fountain hides and splashes
Within this living bread that is life to us
    although it is the night.

I am repining for that living fountain.
Within this bread of life I see it plain
    although it is the night.

RICHARD STANIHURST
(1545-1618)

A Prayer to the Trinitie

Trinitec blessed, deitee coequal,
Unitie sacred, God one eeke in essence.
Yield to they servaund, pitifullye calling,
     Merciful hearing.

Vertuus living dyd I long relinquish,
Thy wyl and precepts misirablye scorning,
Graunt toe mee, sinful pacient, repenting,
     Helthful amendment.

Blessed I judge him, that in hart is healed:
Cursed I know him, that in helth is harmed:
Thy physick therefore, toe me, wretch unhappye,
     Send mye Redeemer.

Glorye toe God, the Father, and his onlye
Soon, the protectoure of us earthlye sinners,
Thee sacred Spirit, laborers refreshing,
     Still be renowned. Amen.

GEOFFREY KEATING
(1570-1650)

Translation by Padraig Pearse

Keen Thyself, Poor Wight

Keen thyself, poor wight:
From weeping others restrain thine eyes;
Keen not daughter, keen not son
That hath been shrouded in clay.

Keen first thine own sin
Ere thy body goeth into dust;
Keen, since thou must pay for it,
The passion Christ suffered for thy sake.

Keen the sufferings on thy behalf
Of Christ, Who redeemed all upon a tree,
Keen His two hands and His two feet,
And His heart which the blind man clave.

Every single one shall go:
Yet keen none that shall pass from thee,—
Beyond all that have ever been laid in earth,
Thine own case, poor wretch, toucheth thee most nearly.

Of all that the Creator's right hand hath made,
Of boys, of women and of men,
There is none, weak or mighty,
But shall pass unto his death.

Couldst thou see all that have gone from thee,
As these hosts beneath us are,
Before all that have ever gone into earth,
Thou wouldst keen thyself first.

On Sion hill, on the day of the hosts,
Thy face shall be blacker than a coal,
Though fair thy aspect now —
Unless thou keen thyself while here.

Since death is the messenger of God,
Shouldst thou repine at his doings,
Thou wouldst achieve thine own misfortune
And the misfortune of him that hath gone.

Alas, poor witless wight,
Didst thou understand thyself as thou art,
Thou wouldst cease to keen for others
And yet wouldst be weeping forever!

LUKE WADDING
(1588-1657)

Christmas Day is come

Christmas Day is come; let's all prepare for mirth,
  Which fills the heav'ns and earth at this amazing birth.
Through both the joyous angels in strife and hurry fly,
  With glory and hosannas, 'All Holy' do they cry.
In heaven the Church triumphant adores with all her choirs,
  The militant on earth with humble faith admires.

But why should we rejoice? Should we not rather mourn
  To see the Hope of Nations thus in a stable born?
Where are His crown and sceptre, where is His throne sublime,
  Where is His train majestic that should the stars outshine?
Is there not sumptuous palace nor any inn at all
  To lodge His heav'nly mother but in a filthy stall?

GEOFFREY MAC BRIAIN MAC AN BHAIRD
(c. 1600)

Translation by the sixth Earl of Longford

Morning Prayer

Lord, aid my work this day,
    And guide my feet aright
From learning's idle tricks away
    To innocence and light.

Thou plainly seest my needs.
    My wandering wits confine,
Be in my heart, work in my deeds,
    Make strong my strength with Thine.

Death by Thy Death is dead,
    With Thee in joy I stay.
Thy shield of grace above me spread,
    Protect me thro' the day!

RICHARD FLECKNOE
(1600-1678)

On the Death of Our Lord

Oh blessed Lord! and wouldst thou die
For such a wretched worm as I!
This of thy love's so great a proof,
Angels can ne'er admire enough;
And all the love by far transcends
Of parents and of dearest friends.
To have such benefit bestow'd
Would undo any but a God;
And love itself make bankrupt too,
By leaving nothing more to do.
Had any king done this for me,
What wondering at it there would be!
And wondering at it now there's none
When by a God himself 'tis done.
Strange blindness! man should more esteem
A benefit bestowed on him
By earthly kings, than what is given
Unto him by the King of Heaven!

ROGER BOYLE, EARL OF ORRERY
(1621 - 1679)

On Christmas Day

Hail, glorious day which miracles adorn,
Since 'twas on thee eternity was born!
Hail, glorious day, on which mankind did view
The Saviour of the old world and the new!

Hail, glorious day, which deifies man's race,
Birth-day of Jesus and, through him, of grace!
In thy blest light the world at once did see
Proofs of his Godhead and humanity.

To prove him man, he did from woman come,
To prove him God, 'twas from a virgin's womb.
Man ne'er could feign, what his strange birth prov'd true,
For his blest mother was a virgin too.

While as a child he in the manger cries,
Angels proclaim his Godhead from the skyes;
He to so vile a cradle did submit,
That we, through faith in him, on thrones might sit.

Oh prodigie of mercy, which did make
The God of Gods our human nature take!
And through our vaile of flesh, his glory shine,
That we thereby might share in the divine.

Hail, glorious virgin, whose tryumphant womb
Blesses all ages past and all to come!
Thou more than heal'st the sin of Adam's wife,
She brought in death, but thou brought'st endless life.

No wonder in the world could be,
Than thou to live in it and heaven in thee.
All generations still shall call thee blest.
To thee that title is most justly paid,
Since by thy Son we sons of God are made!

FEAR DORCHA O MEALLAIN
(c. 1650)

Translation by Thomas Kinsella

Little is known of O Mealláin *except that he was probably a native of Co. Down, and may have been a priest.* An Act of Parliament passed in 1652, following Cromwell's campaign in Ireland, aimed at the dispossesison of the British Parliament's defeated enemies east of the Shannon. The prayer in the first stanza of O Mealláin's poem is a version of a prayer said traditionally before undertaking a journey. His comparison between the plight of the Irish and that of 'Israel's people' is a commonplace of seventeenth century poetry.

Exodus to Connacht

In the name of the Father full of virtue,
    in the name of the Son Who suffered pain,
in the name of the Holy Ghost in power,
    Mary and her Son be with us.

Our sole possessions: Michael of miracles,
    the virgin Mary, the twelve apostles,
Brigid, Patrick and Saint John
    — and fine rations: faith in God.

Sweet Colm Cille of miracles too,
    and Colmán Mac Aoidh, poets' patron,
will all be with us on our way.
    Do not bewail our journey West.

Brothers mine, do you not see
    the ways of the world a while now?
However much we may possess
    we'll go with little into the grave.

Consider a parable of this:
    Israel's people, God's own,
although they were in bonds in Egypt,
    found in time a prompt release.

Through the mighty sea they passed,
    an ample road was made for them,

then the grey-green ocean rose
   out there above them like a rock.

When they came to dry land
   the King of Heaven minded them
—relief, succour and nourishment
   from the God Who ever was and is.

Food from Heaven they received:
   great wheat, in no small measure,
honey settling like a mist,
   abundant water out of rock.

Likewise it shall be done to you:
   all good things shall first be yours.
Heaven is your inheritance.
   Be not faint-hearted in your faith.

People of my heart, stand steady,
   don't complain of your distress.
Moses got what he requested,
   religious freedom — and from Pharaoh.

Identical their God and ours.
   One God there was and still remains.
Here or Westward God is one,
   one God ever and shall be.

If they call you 'Papishes'
   accept it gladly for a title.
Patience, for the High King's sake.
   Deo Gratias, good the name!

God Who art generous, O Prince of Blessings,
   behold the Gael, stripped of authority.
Now as we journey Westward into Connacht
   Old friends we'll leave behind us in their grief.

LUKE WADDINGE

(Died 1691)

For Christmas Day

This Christmas Day you pray me sing,
My Carol to our new-born King,
A God made Man, the Virgin's Son,
The Word made Flesh, can this be done?
  Of me I pray no more require
  Then this great Mystery to admire.

Whom Heaven of Heavens cannot contain,
As Scripture doth declare most plain,
In a poor stable is born this day
Lay'd in a manger wrapt in hay.
  Of me I pray no more require
  Then this great Mystery to admire.

Heaven's great treasures are now but small!
Immensity no extent at all,
Eternity's but one day old
Tho' Almighty feeleth the Winter cold,
  Of me I pray no more require
  Then this great Mystery to admire.

For Saint Stephen's Day

Saint Stephen had an angel's face
All full of virtue, full of grace,
By the false Jews was stoned to death,
For Jesus Christ and for his faith;
  But for those stones in Heaven he found
  Of precious pearls a glorious crown.

The Jews do falsely him accuse
And in their council him abuse,

Their furious rage without delay
Make stones their arms him to destroy;
    But for those stones in Heaven he found
    Of precious pearls a glorious crown.

The most sweet saint with his last breath
Doth pray for those who seek his death,
And leaves not off whilst life doth last,
As thick as hail their stones to cast;
    And for those stones in Heaven he found
    Of precious pearls a glorious crown.

For Saint John's Day

Saint John did lean on Jesus's breast,
Jesus loved John more than the rest,
Our loving Jesus St John did love,
His Gospel it doth clearly prove,
    Then let St John be loved by us
    Who was beloved by our Jesus.

Divine mysteries locked under seal
To St John Jesus did reveal,
His secrets did to him impart,
Made him the treasurer of his heart;
    Then let St John be loved by us
    Who was beloved by our Jesus.

He was Disciple, Evangelist,
Apostle, Prophet, what he list;
John his most darling friend
Jesus to his Mother did commend.
    Then let St John be loved by us
    Who was beloved by our Jesus.

For Innocents' Day

The Angel saith to Joseph mild
Fly with the Mother and the Child,
Out of this land to Egypt go,
The Heavenly Babe will have it so;
    For that his hour is not yet come,
    To die for Man's Redemption.

Proud Herod he doth froth and frown
Feareth to lose Kingdom and Crown,
Full of distain and full of scorn,
He must destroy this young King born;
    But stay, his hour is not yet come
    To die for Man's Redemption.

Herod, forbear this cruel flood
Of the most pure innocent Blood,
To thee a crown this Child doth bring
To make thee happier than a king;
    From highest Heavens along he's come
    To die for Man's Redemption.

For Twelfth Day

Behold three Kings come from the East
Led by a Star of stars the best,
Which brought them where they did espy
The King of Kings and Saviour lie;
    With gold and myrrh and frankincense
    They do adore this new-born Prince.

It's strange what did these three Kings see
That might by them adored be,
A tender Babe laid on the ground,
Yet they submit sceptre and crown;
    Their gold, their myrrh, their frankincense
    For to adore this new-born Prince.

Then let us with those three Kings bring
Our gifts unto this new-born King;
Our sense, our will, our wit, our heart,
And all that e'er we can impart;
    Our gold, our myrrh, our frankincense,
    For to adore the new-born Prince.

NAHUM TATE
(1652-1715)

While Shepherds watched Their Flocks

While shepherds watched their flocks by night,
    All seated on the ground,
The angel of the Lord came down,
    And glory shone around.

'Fear not,' said he, for mighty dread
    Had seized their troubled mind;
'Glad tidings of great joy I bring
    To you and all mankind.

'To you, in David's town, this day
    Is born of David's line,
The Saviour, who is Christ the Lord,
    And this shall be the sign:

The Heavenly babe you there shall find
    To human view displayed,
All meanly wrapped in swaddling bands,
    And in a manger laid.'

Thus spake the seraph; and forthwith
    Appeared a shining throng
Of angels, praising God, who thus
    Addressed their joyful song:

'All glory be to God on high,
    And to the earth be peace;
Good will henceforth from Heaven to men
    Begin and never cease.'

Lord, have Mercy

Have mercy, Lord, on me,
　　As thou wert ever kind;
Let me, opprest with load of guilt,
　　Thy wonted mercy find.

Wash off my foul offence
　　And cleanse me from my sin;
For I confess my crime, and see
　　How great my guilt has been.

The joy thy favour gives
　　Let me again obtain,
And thy free Spirit's firm support
　　My fainting soul sustain.

To God the Father, Son,
　　And Spirit glory be,
As 'twas, and is, and shall be so
　　To all eternity. Amen.

As pants the Hart

As pants the hart for cooling streams
　　When heated in the chase,
So longs my soul, O God, for thee,
　　And thy refreshing grace.

For thee, my God, the living God,
　　My thirsty soul doth pine:
O when shall I behold thy face,
　　Thou Majesty divine?

Why restless, why cast down, my soul?
　　Hope still, and thou shalt sing
The praise of him who is thy God,
　　Thy health's eternal spring.

To Father, Son, and Holy Ghost,
    The God whom we adore,
Be glory, as it was, is now,
    And shall be evermore.

JONATHAN SWIFT
(1667-1745)

On a Curate's Complaint of Hard Duty

I march'd three miles through scorching sand,
With zeal in heart, and notes in hand;
I rode four more to Great St Mary,
Using four legs when two were weary:
To three fair virgins I did tie men,
In the close bands of pleasing Hymen;
I dipp'd two babes in holy water,
And purified their mother after.
Within an hour and eke a half,
I preach'd three congregations deaf;
Where, thundering out, with lungs long-winded,
I chopp'd so fast, that few were minded.
My emblem, the laborious sun,
Saw all these mighty labours done
Before one race of his was run.
All this perform'd by Robert Hewit:
What mortal else could e'er go through it!

PIARAS MAC GEARAILT
(1709-1791)

Translation by Joan Keefe

An accomplished poet in Irish, Piaras MacGearailt (Pierce Fitzgerald) was leader or 'High-Sheriff' of a famous Court of Poetry that was convened a few times in his home district near Youghal. The Fitzgeralds had once owned large estates but most had been confiscated by the time Piaras inherited. To save the last remnants he chose to give up his Catholic religion and turn Protestant. This provoked an attack in verse by one Thomas Barry, a poet of Clonmel. 'To Thomas Barry' is Piaras MacGearailt's reply.

An Answer to Thomas Barry

Dearest Barry,
My clever friend,
Going over to Calvin
Is my cross to carry
Because my children's loss
Of acres and herds
Left my life a stormy
Heartstream of tears.

Too long has this wrong
Lain on our chiefs,
They are rent, impoverished
And crushed into weakness.
Bright God, if you don't trample
On these foreign boors
Soon all our landowners
Will follow my sad move.

This is a sickness and hurt
Wounding me, never
Ceasing cutting to
My lungs and my liver,
That rather than my children
Be sunk in the dirt
I drew strife on my soul
For love of earth.

73

Do not harbour anger
In your minds for me,
Enough that Heaven's wrath
Is launched, my friends,
And to guard my soul
I urge the Son of God;
Though I am a sinner
Sunk in the world's mire,
Fettered in the world's chains,
Still to the mild nurse
Of Christ I cry
'Dispel my sighs,
Relieve me of this curse!'

My faith has done me harm
In a way that is not fitting,
And to avoid it for land
Cannot be a proper thing.
I claim it is unfair
And pray now without fail
For help from the unchanging King.

O dear friend, remember
I was a creature cornered,
Though to your mind
Merely a man deluded,
But fines and rent and tax
And costs of litigation
Made many more than me
Cross the road to Luther.

TADHG GAELACH O SUILLEABHAIN
(1715-1795)

Translation by Thomas Kinsella

A Poem to the Heart of Jesus

The light in my heart, O Saviour, is Thy heart,
the wealth of my heart, Thy heart poured out for me.
Seeing that Thy heart, Love, filled with love for me
leave Thy heart in keeping, hooded in mine.

The pains we have caused Thee, bright high King of the Powers,
their nature and number, truly my mind cannot hold.
The noxious hot hurt in Thy heart and Thy wound, O Love,
sweetly hurried the just in thousands to their Crown.

Father and Jesus, Whose death has saved my life,
Who fashioned my face in Thy form, without craftsman's toil,
is it not barbarous, Christ, I have yet not loved
save in those matters Thou holdest in disgust?

What Moses received of Thy law, on the hosts' behalf,
my heart was not often at peace with, nor content
— but gluttony, greed, spite and venomous rage,
reviling of men, and thousands of sins more serious.

Weary with sorrow for what I have done, I will go
to journey all parts of the land of Fáilbhe and Eoghan
confessing my deeds and mourning with cries of grief,
wailing in woe for it all, and shedding tears.

And when I return and have prayed to Thee, Flower of the Orders,
in the refuge of Christ, with the guard of His grace about me,
the harsh stony heathery hills that troubled me once
will alter to silk smooth plains and pastures of satin.

The Knot

Holy bright King, although Thou hadst strayed from Heaven

tormented amongst us in ways that can never be measured,
Thy love Thou hadst hidden, O Christ, till the lance tore
a mansion secure in Thy heart for the whole world.

OLIVER GOLDSMITH
(1728-1774)

The Village Preacher
From *The Deserted Village*

Near yonder copse, where once the garden smiled,
And still where many a garden flower grows wild;
There, where a few torn shrubs the place disclose,
The village preacher's modest mansion rose.
A man he was to all the country dear,
And passing rich with forty pounds a year;
Remote from towns he ran his godly race,
Nor e'er had changed, nor wished to change his place;
Unpractised he to fawn, or seek for power,
by doctrines fashioned to the varying hour;
Far other aims his heart had learned to prize,
More skilled to raise the wretched than to rise.
His house was known to all the vagrant train,
He chid their wanderings, but relieved their pain;
The long-remembered beggar was his guest,
Whose beard descending swept his aged breast;
The ruined spendthrift, now no longer proud,
Claimed kindred here, and had his claim allowed.
The broken soldier, kindly bade to stay,
Sat by his fire, and talked the night away,
Wept o'er his wounds, or, tales of sorrow done,
Shouldered his crutch and showed how fields were won.
Pleased with his guests, the good man learned to glow,
And quite forgot their vices in their woe;
Careless their merits or their faults to scan,
His pity gave ere charity began.

Thus to relieve the wretched was his pride,
And even his failings leaned to virtue's side;
But in his duty prompt at every call,
He watch'd and wept, he pray'd and felt for all.
And, as a bird each fond endearment tries
To tempt its new-fledg'd offspring to the skies,

He tried each art, reprov'd each dull delay,
Allur'd to brighter worlds, and led the way.

Beside the bed where parting life was laid,
And sorrow, guilt and pain by turns dismay'd,
The reverend champion stood. At his control,
Despair and anguish fled the struggling soul;
Comfort came down the trembling wretch to raise,
And his last falt'ring accents whisper'd praise.

At church, with meek and unaffected grace,
His looks adorn'd the venerable place;
Truth from his lips prevailed with double sway,
And fools, who came to scoff, remained to pray.
The service past, around the pious man
With steady zeal, each honest rustic ran;
Even the children follow'd with endearing wile,
And pluck'd his gown to share the good man's smile.
His ready smile a parent's warmth express'd,
Their welfare pleas'd him, and their cares distress'd;
To them his heart, his love, his griefs were given,
But all his serious thoughts had rest in heaven.
As some tall cliff that lifts its awful form,
Swells from the vale, and midway leaves the storm,
Though round its breast the rolling clouds are spread,
Eternal sunshine settles on its head.

CONOR O'RIORDAN
(c. 1750)

Translation by Eleanor Hull

Hymn to the Virgin Mary

Queen of all Queens, oh! Wonder of the loveliness of women,
Heart which hath held in check for us the righteous wrath of God;
Strong Staff of Light, and Fosterer of the Bright Child of Heaven,
Pray thou for us as we now pray that we may be forgiven.

She of the King of Stars beloved, stainless, undefiled,
Christ chose as His Mother-nurse, to Him, the stainless Child;
Within her breast, as in a nest, the Paraclete reposes,
Lily among fairest flowers, Rose amid red roses.

She, the bright unsheathed sword to guard our souls in anguish,
She, the flawless limber-branch, to cover those that languish;
Where her healing mantle flows, may I find my hiding,
'Neath the fringes of her robe constantly abiding.

Hostile camps upon the plain, sharp swords clashed together,
Stricken fleets across the main stressed by wintry weather;
Weary sickness on my heart, sinful thoughts alluring,
All the fever of my soul clings to her for curing.

She the Maid the careful king of the wide wet world chooses,
In her speech forgiveness lies, no suppliant she refuses;
White Star of our troubled sea, on thy name I'm crying,
That Christ may draw in His spread net the living and the dying.

Lament for Timoleague

Lone and weary as I wander'd by the bleak shore of the sea,
Meditating and reflecting on the world's hard destiny,
Forth the moon and stars 'gan glimmer, in the quiet tide beneath,
For on slumbering spring and blossom breathed not out of heaven
    a breath.

On I went in sad dejection, careless where my footsteps bore,
Till a ruined church before me opened wide its ancient door, —
Till I stood before the portals, where of old were wont to be,
For the blind, the halt, and leper, alms and hospitality.

Still the ancient seat was standing, built against the buttress grey,
Where the clergy used to welcome weary trav'llers on their way;
There I sat me down in sadness, 'neath my cheek I placed my hand,
Till the tears fell hot and briny down upon the grassy land.

There, I said in woeful sorrow, weeping bitterly the while,
Was a time when joy and gladness reigned within this ruined pile; —
Was a time when bells were tinkling, clergy preaching peace abroad,
Psalms a-singing, music ringing praises to the mighty God.

Empty aisle, deserted chancel, tower tottering to your fall,
Many a storm since then has beaten on the grey head of your wall!
Many a bitter storm and tempest has your roof-tree turned away,
Since you first were formed a temple to the Lord of night and day.

Holy house of ivied gables, that were once the country's boast,
Houseless now in weary wandering are you scattered, saintly host;
Lone you are today, and dismal, — joyful psalms no more are heard,
Where, within your choir, her vesper screeches the cat-headed bird.

Ivy from your eaves is growing, nettles round your green hearthstone,
Winds howl where, in your corners, dropping waters make their moan.

Where the lark to early matins used your clergy forth to call,
There, alas! no tongue is stirring, save the dawn upon the wall.

Refectory cold and empty, dormitory bleak and bare;
Whence are now your pious uses, simple bed and frugal fare?
Gone your abbot, rule, and order, broken down your altar stones;
Nought I see beneath your shelter, save a heap of clayey bones.

Oh! the hardship — oh! the hatred, tyranny and cruel war,
Persecution and oppression that have left you as you are!
I myself once also prospered; — mine is, too, an altered plight;
Trouble, care and age have left me good for nought but grief tonight.

Gone, my motion and my vigour — gone the use of eye and ear;
At my feet lie friends and children, powerless and corrupting here;
Woe is written on my visage, in a nut my heart would lie —
Death's deliverance were welcome — Father, let the old man die.

WILLIAM DRENNAN
(1754-1820)

William Orr was a Presbyterian farmer of Co. Down and a member of the United Irishmen. He was tried for high treason and sentenced to be hanged. His trial was a travesty of justice and outraged public opinion, but the sentence was carried out.

The Wake of William Orr

There our murdered brother lies;
Wake him not with woman's cries;
Mourn the way that manhood ought —
Sit in silent trance of thought.

Write his merits on your mind;
Morals pure and manners kind;
In his head, as on a hill,
Virtue placed her citadel.

Why cut off in palmy youth?
Truth he spoke, and acted truth.
'Countrymen, UNITE,' he cried
And died for what our Saviour died.

God of peace and God of love!
Let it not Thy vengeance move —
Let it not Thy lightnings draw —
A nation guillotined by law.

Hapless Nation, rent and torn,
Thou wert early taught to mourn;
Warfare of six hundred years!
Epochs marked with blood and tears!

Hunted thro' thy native grounds,
Or flung *reward* to human hounds,
Each one pulled or tore his share,
Heedless of thy deep despair.

Hapless Nation! hapless Land!
Heap of uncementing sand!
Crumbled by a foreign weight:
And by worse, domestic hate.

God of mercy! God of peace!
Make this mad confusion cease;
O'er the mental chaos move,
Through it SPEAK the light of love.

Monstrous and unhappy sight!
Brothers' blood will not unite;
Holy oil and holy water
Mix, and fill the world with slaughter.

Who is she with aspect wild?
The widow'd mother with her child —
Child new stirring in the womb!
Husband waiting for the tomb!

Angel of this sacred place,
Calm her soul and whisper peace—
Cord, or axe, or guillotine,
Make the sentence — not the sin.

Here we watch our brother's sleep:
Watch with us, but do not weep:
Watch with us thro' dead of night —
But expect the morning light.

THOMAS MOORE
(1779-1852)

Thy Heaven

Thy heaven, on which 'tis bliss to look,
Shall be my pure and shining book,
Where I shall read, in words of flame,
The glories of thy wondrous name.

There's nothing bright, above, below,
From flowers that bloom to stars that glow,
But in its light my soul can see
Some feature of thy deity:

There's nothing dark, below, above,
But in its gloom I trace thy love,
And meekly wait the moment when
Thy touch shall turn all bright again.

The Irish Peasant to His Mistress

Addressed to the Irish Catholic Church which suffered persecution under penal laws.

Through grief and through danger thy smile hath cheered my way,
Till hope seemed to bud from each thorn that round me lay;
The darker our fortune, the brighter our pure love burned,
Till shame into glory, till fear into zeal was turned;
Yes, slave as I was, in thy arms my spirit felt free,
And blessed even the sorrows that made me more dear to thee.

Thy rival was honoured while thou wert wronged and scorned,
Thy crown was of briars, while gold her brows adorned;
She wooed me to temples whilst thou layest hid in caves,
Her friends were all master while thine, alas! were slaves;
Yet cold in the earth, at thy feet, I would rather be,
Than wed what I loved not, or turn one thought from thee.

They slander thee sorely who say thy vows are frail —
Hadst thou been a false one thy cheek had looked less pale.
They say, too, so long thou hast worn these lingering chains,
That deep in thy heart they have printed their servile stains —
Oh, foul is the slander, — no chains could that soul subdue —
Where shineth *thy* spirit, there liberty shineth, too.

The Bird let loose

The bird let loose in Eastern skies,
    When hasting fondly home,
Ne'er stoops to earth her wing, nor flies
    Where idle warblers roam,
But high she shoots through air and light
    Above all low delay,
Where nothing earthly bounds her flight,
    Nor shadow dims her way.

So grant me, God, from every care,
    And stain of passion free,
Aloft, through virtue's purer air,
    To hold my course to Thee!
No sin to cloud — no lure to stay
    My soul as home she springs; —
Thy sunshine on her jovial way,
    Thy freedom in her wings!

EATON STANNARD BARRETT
(1786-1820)

Woman

Not she with traitorous kiss her Saviour stung,
Not she denied Him with unholy tongue;
She, while apostles shrank, could dangers brave,
Last at the cross and earliest at the grave.

SIR AUBREY DE VERE
(1788-1846)

The Right Use of Prayer

Therefore, when thou wouldst pray, or dost thine alms,
    Blow not a trump before thee. Hyprocrites
    Do thus vaingloriously: the common streets
Boast of their largess, echoing their psalms.
On such the laud of men like unctuous balms
    Falls with sweet savour. Impious Counterfeits!
    Prating of Heaven, for earth their bosom beats:
Grasping at weeds they lose immortal palms.

God needs not iteration nor vain cries;
    That Man communion with his God might share
    Below, Christ gave the ordinance of prayer.
Vague ambages and witless ecstasies
    Avail not. Ere a voice to prayer be given
    The heart should rise on wings of love to Heaven.

HENRY FRANCIS LYTE
(1793-1847)

Abide with Me

Abide with me; fast falls the even-tide;
The darkness deepens; Lord, with me abide!
When other helpers fail, and comforts flee,
Help of the helpless, O abide with me!

Swift to its close ebbs out life's little day!
Earth's joys grow dim, its glories pass away;
Change and decay in all around I see;
O Thou, Who changest not, abide with me!

I need Thy presence ev'ry passing hour;
What but Thy Grace can foil the tempter's power?
Who like Thyself my guide and stay can be?
Through cloud and sunshine, Lord abide with me!

I fear no foe with Thee at hand to bless;
Ills have no weight, and tears no bitterness;
Where is death's sting? Where, grave, thy victory?
I triumph still, if Thou abide with me!

Hold Thou Thy Cross before my closing eyes:
Shine through the gloom, and point me to the skies;
Heaven's morning breaks, and earth's vain shadows flee;—
In life, in death, O Lord abide with me!

ANONYMOUS
(Date unknown)

Translation by Jeremiah J. Callanan

Lines to the Blessed Sacrament

Thou dear and mystic semblance,
    Before whose form I kneel,
I tremble as I think upon
    The glory Thou dost veil,
And ask myself, can he who late
    The ways of darkness trod,
Meet face to face, and heart to heart,
    His sin-avenging God?

My Judge and my Creator,
    If I presume to stand
Amid thy pure and holy ones,
    It is at thy command,
To lay before thy mercy's seat
    My sorrows and my fears,
To wail my life and kiss thy feet
    In silence and in tears.

O God! that dreadful moment,
    In sickness and in strife,
When death and hell seem'd watching
    For the last weak pulse of life,
When on the waves of sin and pain
    My drowning soul was toss'd,
Thy hand of mercy saved me then,
    When hope itself was lost.

I hear thy voice, my Saviour,
    It speaks within my breast,
'Oh, come to me, thou weary one,
    I'll hush thy cares to rest;'

Then from the parched and burning waste
Of sin, where long I trod,
I come to thee, thou stream of life,
My Saviour and my God!

ANONYMOUS
(Traditional Poems)

Translations by Douglas Hyde

The Joyce's Repentance

I am a sinful man of men,
Sin's iron pen my feet have trod,
No single inch in me is whole
So long my soul hath fought with God.

Just when I think my soul to win,
I sin some sin, or lie some lie,
As ducks will leave the clearest springs
To daub their wings in pools half dry.

The fight with Death is hard and long;
(Though Death is strong his pace is slow),
Like helpless ships we turn and toss
And drift across the waves of woe.

Upon this hinge hangs all my dole,
My pain of soul, my bitter smart,
That I have warred with Him who brought
Me out of naught — rebellious heart!

Once I was good, I once was pure,
Whilst yet the lure of sin lay hid;
But as I, ripening, slowly grew,
I lusted too for things forbid.

Gluttony, sloth, distemper, greed,
    Led me with speed the deathly way,
    Envy and anger, lust and strife
    Made of my life their hideous prey.

O man, my warning take to thee,
    That health shall flee, that youth shall part,
    That as I am, thou yet shalt be,
    But ne'er again as now thou art.

I too was strong, I lived in peace
    Until my lease of strength went by;
    A faggot, now, of wearied bones,
    Upon the stones of death I lie.

Night Prayer

I lie down with Thee, O Jesus
    And lie Thou down with me,
That the holy Creed above my head
    And the oil of Christ on my soul may be.

    O Father who sought me,
    O Son who bought me,
    O Holy Spirit who taught me!

O Queen of whiteness,
    Of brightness, of youth,
Lift me from sinning
    And show me the truth.
In my heart put repentance
    And sorrow and ruth.

And if this be my story
    E're morning to die,
May my soul be·in glory
    With God upon high.

Blessed be the Holy Will of God

The will of God be done by us,
The law of God be kept by us,
Our evil will controlled by us,
Our tongue in cheek be held by us,
Repentance timely made by us,
Christ's passion understood by us,
Each sinful crime be shunned by us,
Much on the *End* be mused by us,
And Death be blessed found by us,
With Angel's music heard by us,
And God's high praises sung by us,
For ever and for aye.

Christmas Hymn

Hail to thee thou holy Babe
    In the manger now so poor,
Yet so rich Thou art I ween,
    High within the highest door.

Little babe who art so great,
    Child so young who art so old,
In the manger small his room
    Whom not heaven itself could hold.

Motherless, with mother here,
    Fatherless, a tiny span,
Ever God in heaven's height,
    First to-night becoming man.

Father — not more old than thou!
    Mother — younger, can it be!
Older, younger is the Son,
    Younger, older, she than he.

The Graces of the Holy Ghost

May the grace of the Holy Ghost be gained by us,
And the true Faith be kept unstained by us,
While we follow the path of the saints, endeavouring
To walk in the temple of Christ unwavering.

And may we seek the eternal Trinity
Trusting in Christ and in Christ's divinity,
Helping the poor and relieving them
Walking with God and receiving them.

Devils that tempt us, still repelling them,
All our faults — to the Church confessing them.
Fighting with all that wounds, with energy,
Ceasing from lies and evil calumny.

Let us not mix with strife and devilry,
Fall we to prayer instead of revelry,
Thanking the Lord for all his graciousness
Throwing aside our evil ways from us.

Striving to reach the heaven's holiness,
Paying all debts in peace and lowliness,
Toning the mind to true tranquility,
Saying 'confiteor,' with humility.

Watching for pardon through God's own graciousness.
Taking the Sacrament He has made for us.
Blessings of God and of men still nerving us,
Help of apostles and saints preserving us.

Blessings of Mary and Joseph guiding us,
Making death blessed when life is parting us,
The angels calling with voice of graciousness,
The ladies of Mary making place for us.

Waiting the coming of peace and righteousness,
God's own countenance shining bright on us,
Praising and loving God for aye
Through worlds of worlds in endless day.   Amen.

The Merry Jovial Beggar

I have no more a golden store — this sets the world a-scorning,
Yet I be happy every night and merry every morning.
Each day my bread I ask of God, He sends me not away,
So I shall always merry be, till I be laid in clay.

I thank Him when I wake me up each morn, as well I may,
He brought me safely through the night and lets me see the day.
I hear each morning precious Mass, a blessed means of grace,
And Jesus Christ I still adore within His sacred place.

Upon the roads I pray my prayer, my thanks to God I pour,
Good prayers I have upon my tongue to say at every door.
No fear have I the night to pass, exposed to winter's rigour,
For every house will welcome me, the merry jovial beggar.

I ask no bed, no sheet, no quilt — a wisp of straw lay down
And I shall sleep as sound and deep as kings on beds of down.
I dream of Heaven, the glorious home where angels walk in white,
My guardian angel at my side will watch me through the night.

I seek no gold to have or hold, for riches wear not well,
And countless thousands seeking it have cast themselves to hell,
For gold must melt like snow in Lent, before the breath of Spring,
But the soul that courts it, it must die, a low unlovely thing.

ANONYMOUS
(Traditional Poem)

Translation by Padraic Pearse

The Keening of Mary

'O Peter, O Apostle, hast thou seen my bright love ?'
    (M'ochon agus m'ochon o!)
'I saw Him even now in the midst of His foemen.'
    (M'ochon agus m'ochon o!)

'Come hither, two Marys, till ye keen my bright love.'
    (M"ochon agus m'ochon o!)
'What have we to keen unless we keen His bones ?'
    (M'ochon agus m'ochon o!)

'Who is that stately man on the tree of Passion ?'
    (M'ochon agus m'ochon o!)
'Dost thou not know thy Son, O Mother ?'
    (M'ochon agus m'ochon o!)

'And is that the little Son I carried nine months ?
    (M'ochon agus m'ochon o!)
And is that the little Son that was born in the stable ?
    (M'ochon agus m'ochon o!)

And is that the little Son that was nursed on Mary's breast ?'
    (M'ochon agus m'ochon o!)
'Hush, O Mother, and be not sorrowful!'
    (M'ochon agus m'ochon o!)

'And is that the hammer that struck home the nails through Thee ?
    (M'ochon agus m'ochon o!)
And is that the spear that went through Thy white side ?
    (M'ochon agus m'ochon o!)

'And is that the crown of thorns that crowned Thy beauteous head ?'
    (M'ochon agus m'ochon o!)
'Hush, O Mother, and be not sorrowful!
    (M'ochon agus m'ochon o!)

'Hush, O Mother, and be not sorrowful!
           (*M'ochon agus m'ochon o*)
The women of My keening are yet unborn, little Mother.'
           (*M'ochon agus m'ochon o!*)

O woman who weepest, by this My death
           (*M'ochon agus m'ochon o*)!
There will be hundreds to-day in the garden of Paradise!'
           (*M'ochon agus m'ochon o!*)

JOHN BANIM
(1798-1842)

Soggarth Aroon

Am I the slave they say,
   Soggarth Aroon?
Since you did show the way,
   Soggarth Aroon,
Their slave no more to be,
While they would work with me
Old Ireland's slavery,
   Soggarth Aroon.

Why not her poorest man,
   Soggarth Aroon,
Try and do all he can,
   Soggarth Aroon,
Her commands to fulfil,
Of his own heart and will,
Side by side with you still,
   Soggarth Aroon?

Loyal and brave to you
   Soggarth Aroon,
Yet be not slave to you
   Soggarth Aroon,
Nor out of fear to you,
Stand up so dear to you,
Och! out of fear to *you*,
   Soggarth Aroon!

Who in the winter's night,
   Soggarth Aroon,
When the cold blast did bite,
   Soggarth Aroon,
Came to my cabin door
And on my earthen floor
Knelt by me, sick and poor,
   Soggarth Aroon?

Who, on the marriage day,
 Soggarth Aroon,
Made the poor cabin gay?
 Soggarth Aroon,
And did both laugh and sing
Making our hearts to ring,
At the poor christening,
 Soggarth Aroon.

Who, as friend only met,
 Soggarth Aroon,
Never did flout me yet,
 Soggarth Aroon,
And when my heart was dim,
Gave, while his eye did brim,
What should I give to him?
 Soggarth Aroon.

Och! you, and only you,
 Soggarth Aroon,
And for this I was true to you,
 Soggarth Aroon,
In love they'll never shake,
When for Old Ireland's sake,
We a true part will take,
 Soggarth Aroon.

GERALD GRIFFIN
(1803-1840)

To a Seagull

White bird of the tempest! O beautiful thing!
With the bosom of snow and the motionless wing,
Now sweeping the billow, now floating on high,
Now bathing thy plumes in the light of the sky!
Now poising o'er ocean thy delicate form,
Now breasting the surge with thy bosom so warm;
Now darting aloft with a heavenly scorn,
Now shooting along like a ray of the morn;
Now lost in the folds of the cloud-curtained dome,
Now floating abroad like a flake of the foam;
Now silently poised o'er the war of the main,
Like the spirit of Charity brooding o'er pain;
Now gliding with pinion all silently furled,
Like an angel descending to comfort the world!
Thou seem'st to my spirit, as upwards I gaze,
And see thee now clothed in mellowest rays,
Now lost in the storm-driven vapours that fly
Like hosts that are routed across the broad sky,
Like a pure spirit true to its virtue and faith,
Mid the tempests of Nature, and passion, and death!

Rise! beautiful emblem of purity, rise
On the sweet winds of Heaven to thine own brilliant skies;
Still higher — still higher — till lost to our sight,
Thou hidest thy wings in a mantle of light;
And I think, how a pure spirit gazing on thee,
Must long for the moment — the joyous and free —
When the soul disembodied from nature shall spring
Unfettered at once to her Maker and King;
When the bright day of service and suffering past,
Shapes fairer than thine shall shine round her at last,
While, the standard of battle triumphantly furled,
She smiles like a victor, serene on the world!

To the Blessed Virgin Mary

As the mute nightingale in closest groves
    Lies hid at noon, but when day's piercing eye
    Is locked in night, with full heart beating high,
Poureth her plain song o'er the light she loves,
So, Virgin, ever pure and ever blest,
    Moon of religion, from whose radiant face,
    Reflected streams the light of heavenly grace
On broken hearts, by contrite thoughts oppressed —
So, Mary, they who justly feel the weight
    Of Heaven's offended majesty, implore
    Thy reconciling aid, with suppliant knee.
Of sinful man, O sinless Advocate!
    To thee they turn, not him the less adore;
'Tis still his light they love, less dreadful seen in thee.

JAMES CLARENCE MANGAN
(1803-1849)

Hymn for Pentecost

Pure Spirit of the always-faithful God,
  Kindler of Heaven's true light within the soul!
From lorn land our sainted fathers trod,
  Ascends to Thee our cry of hope and dole.
    Thee, Thee we praise!
    To Thee we raise
    Our choral hymn in these awakening days:
O, send us down anew that fire
Which of old lived in David's and Isaiah's lyre.

Centuries had rolled, and earth lay tombed in sleep,
  The nightmare sleep of nations beneath kings;
And far abroad o'er liberty's great deep
  Death's angel waved his black and stilling wings.
    Then struck Thine hour!
    Thou, in Thy power,
    But breathedst, and the free stood up, a tower;
And tyranny's thrones and strongholds fell,
And men made jubilee for an abolished hell.

And she, our mother-house, the famed, the fair,
  The golden house of light and intellect,
Must she still groan in her intense despair?
  Shall she lie prone while Europe stands erect?
    Forfend this, Thou
    To Whom we vow
    Souls even our giant wrongs shall never bow:
Thou wilt not leave our green flag furled,
Nor bear that we abide the byword of the world.

Like the last lamp that burned in Tullia's tomb
  Through ages, vainly, with unwaning ray,
Our star of Hope lights but a path of gloom,
  Whose false track leads us round and round alway.

But Thou canst ope
A gate from hope
To victory! Thou canst nerve our arms to cope
With looming storm and danger still,
And lend a thunder-voice to the land's lightning-will.

Descend, then, Spirit of the Eternal King!
To thee, to Him, to His avenging Son,
The Divine God, in boundless trust we cling;
His help once ours, our nationhood is won.
We watch the time
Till that sublime
Event shall thrill the free of every clime.
Speed, mighty Spirit! speed its march,
And thus complete for earth mankind's triumphal arch.

Gone in the Wind

Solomon! where is thy throne? It is gone in the wind.
Babylon! where is thy might? It is gone in the wind.
Like the swift shadows of Noon, like the dreams of the Blind,
Vanish the glories and pomps of the earth in the wind.

Man! canst thou build upon aught in the pride of thy mind?
Wisdom will teach thee that nothing can tarry behind;
Though there be thousand bright actions embalmed and enshrined,
Myriads and millions of brighter are snow in the wind.

Solomon! where is thy throne? It is gone in the wind.
Babylon! where is thy might? It is gone in the wind.
All that the genius of Man hath achieved or designed
Waits but its hour to be dealt with as dust by the wind.

Say, what is Pleasure? A phantom, a mask undefined;
Science? An almond, whereof we can pierce but the rind;
Honour and Affluence? Firmans that Fortune has signed
Only to glitter and pass on the wings of the wind.

Solomon! where is thy throne? It is gone in the wind.
Babylon! where is thy might? It is gone in the wind.
Who is the Fortunate? He who in anguish hath pined;
He shall rejoice when his relics are dust in the wind.

Mortal! be careful with what thy best hopes are entwined;
Woe to the miners of Truth — where the Lampless have mined!
Woe to the seekers on earth for — what none ever find!
They and their trust shall be scattered like leaves on the wind.

Solomon, where is thy throne? It is gone in the wind.
Babylon! where is thy might? It is gone in the wind.
Happy in death are they only whose hearts have consigned
All Earth's affections and longings and cares to the wind.

Pity, thou reader! the madness of poor Humankind,
Raving of Knowledge, — and Satan so busy to blind!
Raving of Glory,— like me, — for the garlands I bind
(Garlands of song) are but gathered, and — strewn in the wind!

Solomon, where is thy throne? It is gone in the wind.
Babylon! where is thy might? It is gone in the wind.
I Abul-Namez, must rest; for my fire hath declined,
And I hear vioces from Hades like bells on the wind.

SIR WILLIAM ROWAN HAMILTON
(1805-1865)

O Brooding Spirit

O Brooding Spirit of Wisdom and of Love,
Whose mighty wings even now o'ershadow me,
Absorb me in thine own immensity,
And raise me far my finite self above!
Purge vanity away, and the weak care
That name or fame of me may widely spread:
And the deep wish keep burning in their stead,
Thy blissful influence afar to bear,
Or see it borne! Let no desire of ease,
No lack of courage, faith, or love, delay
Mine own steps on that high thought-paven way,
In which my soul her dear commission sees:
Yet with an equal joy let me behold
Thy chariot o'er that way by others rolled!

RICHARD CHENEVIX TRENCH
(1807-1886)

Sonnet

Lord, what a change within us one short hour
Spent in thy presence will prevail to make,
What heavy burdens from our bosoms take,
What parched grounds refresh, as with a shower!
We kneel, and all around us seems to lower;
We rise, and all, the distant and the near,
Stands forth in sunny outline, brave and clear;
We kneel how weak, we rise how full of power.
Why therefore should we do ourselves this wrong
Or others — that we are not always strong,
That we are ever overborne with care,
That we should ever weak or heartless be,
Anxious or troubled, when with us is prayer,
And joy and strength and courage are with Thee?

JOHN KEEGAN
(1809-1849)

Irish Reaper's Harvest Hymn

All hail! Holy Mary, our hope and our joy!
Smile down, blessed Queen! on the poor Irish boy
Who wanders away from his dear beloved home;
O Mary! be with me wherever I roam.
    Be with me, O Mary!
    Forsake me not, Mary!

From the home of my fathers in anguish I go,
To toil for the dark-livered, cold-hearted foe,
Who mocks me, and hates me, and calls me a slave,
An alien, a savage — all names but a knave.
    But, blessed be Mary!
    My sweet, holy Mary!
The *bodagh* he never dare call me a knave.

From my mother's mud sheeling an outcast I fly,
With a cloud on my heart and a tear in my eye.
Oh! I burn as I think what if *Some One* would say,
'Revenge on your tyrants!' — but, Mary! I pray
    From my soul's depth, O Mary!
    And hear me, sweet Mary!
For union and peace to old Ireland I pray.

The land that I fly from is fertile and fair,
And more than I ask or I wish for is there.
But *I* must not taste the good things that I see —
'There's nothing but rags and green rushes for me'
    O mild Virgin Mary!
    O sweet Mother Mary!
Who keeps my rough hand from red murder but thee?

bodagh: a clown or churl

But sure in the end our dear freedom we'll gain,
And wipe from the green flag each Sassanach stain,
And oh! Holy Mary, your blessing we crave!
Give hearts to the timid, and hands to the brave.
     And then, Mother Mary!
     Our own blessed Mary!
Light liberty's flame in the hut of the slave!

SIR SAMUEL FERGUSON
(1810-1846)

The Burial of King Cormac

'Crom Cruach and his sub-gods twelve,'
 Said Cormac, 'are but craven treenc;
The axe that made them, haft or helve,
 Hath worthier of our worship been.

'But He who made the tree to grow,
 And hid in earth the iron-stone,
And made the man with mind to know
 The axe's use, is God alone.'

Anon to priests of Crom was brought —
 Where, girded in their service dread,
They minister'd on red Moy Slaught —
 Word of the words King Cormac said.

They loosed their curse against the king;
 They cursed him in his flesh and bones;
And daily in their mystic ring
 They turn'd the maledictive stones.

Till, where at meat the monarch sate,
 Amid the revel and the wine,
He choked upon the food he ate,
 At Sletty, southward of the Boyne.

High vaunted then the priestly throng,
 And far and wide they noised abroad
With trump and loud liturgic song
 The praise of their avenging God.

But ere the voice was wholly spent
 That priest and prince should still obey,
To awed attendants o'er him bent
 Great Cormac gathered breath to say, —

'Spread not the beds of Brugh for me
    When restless death-bed's use is done:
But bury me at Rossnaree
    And face me to the rising sun.

'For all the kings who lie in Brugh
    Put trust in gods of wood and stone;
And 'twas at Ross that first I knew
    One, Unseen, who is God alone.

'His glory lightens from the east;
    His message soon shall reach our shore;
And idol-god, and cursing priest
    Shall plague us from Moy Slaught no more.'

Dead Cormac on his bier they laid:
    'He reign'd a king for forty years,
And shame it were', his captains said,
    'He lay not with his royal peers.

'His grandsire, Hundred-Battle, sleeps
    Serene in Brugh: and, all around,
Dead kings in stone sepulchral keeps
    Protect the sacred burial ground.

'What though a dying man should rave
    Of changes o'er the eastern sea?
In Brugh of Boyne shall be his grave,
    And not in noteless Rossnaree.'

Then northward forth they bore the bier,
    And down from Sletty side they drew,
With horsemen and with charioteer,
    To cross the fords of Boyne to Brugh.

There came a breath of finer air
    That touched the Boyne with ruffling wings,
It stirr'd him in his sedgy lair
    And in his mossy moorland springs.

And as the burial train came down
    With dirge and savage dolorous shows,
Across their pathway, broad and brown
    The deep, full-hearted river rose;

From bank to bank through all his fords,
    'Neath blackening squalls he swell'd and boil'd;
And thrice the wondering gentile lords
    Essay'd to cross, and thrice recoil'd.

Then forth stepp'd grey-haired warriors four:
    They said, 'Through angrier floods than these,
On link'd shields once our king we bore
    From Dread-Spear and the hosts of Deece.

'And long as loyal will holds good,
    And limbs respond with helpful thews,
Nor flood, not fiend within the flood,
    Shall bar him of his burial dues.'

With slanted necks they stoop'd to lift;
    They heaved him up to neck and chin:
And, pair and pair, with footsteps swift,
    Lock'd arm and shoulder, bore him in.

'Twas brave to see them leave the shore;
    To mark the deep'ning surges rise,
And fall subdued in foam before
    The tension of their striding thighs.

'Twas brave, when now a spear-cast out,
    Breast-high the battling surges ran;
For weight was great, and limbs were stout,
    And loyal man put trust in man.

But ere they reach'd the middle deep,
    Nor steadying weight of clay they bore,
Nor strain of sinewy limbs could keep
    Their feet beneath the swerving four.

And now they slide, and now they swim,
    and now, amid the blackening squall,
Grey locks afloat, with clutching grim,
    They plunge around the floating pall.

While, as a youth with practised spear
    Through justling crowds bears off the ring,
Boyne from their shoulders caught the bier
    And proudly bore away the king.

At morning, on the grassy marge
    Of Rossnaree, the corpse was found,
And shepherds at their early charge
    Entomb'd it in the peaceful ground.

A tranquil spot: a hopeful sound
    Comes from the ever youthful stream,
And still on daisied mead and mound
    The dawn delays with tenderer beam.

Round Cormac Spring renews her buds:
    In march perpetual by her side,
Down come the earth-fresh April floods,
    And up the sea-fresh salmon glide;

And life and time rejoicing run
    From age to age their wonted way;
But still he waits the risen Sun,
    For still 'tis only dawning Day.

JOSEPH SHERIDAN LE FANU
(1814-1873)

Hymn
From *Beatrice*

Hush! oh ye billows,
    Hush! oh thou wind,
Watch o'er us, angels,
    Mary, be kind!

Fishermen followed
    The steps of the Lord;
Oft in their fishing boats
    Preached He the Word.

Pray for us, Pietro,
    Pray for us, John,
Pray for us, Giacomo,
    Zebedee's son.

If it be stormy,
    Fear not the sea;
Jesus upon it
    Is walking by thee.

Billows, be gentle,
    Soft blow the wind,
Watch o'er us, angels,
    Mary, be kind!

Soft be the billows,
    Gentle the wind,
Angels watch over thee,
    Mary, be kind!

AUBREY DE VERE
(1814-1902)

Dominica Pentecostes

The Form decreed of tree and flower
 The Shape susceptible of life
Without the infused, vivific Power
 Were but a slumber or a strife.

He whom the plastic Hand of God
 Himself created out of earth
Remained a statue and a clod
 Till Spirit infused to life gave birth.

So till that hour the Church. In Christ
 Her awful structure, nerve and bone,
Though founded, shaped and organized
 Existed but in skeleton.

Till down on that predestined frame,
 Complete through its sacred mould
That Pentecostal Spirit came,
 The self-same Spirit Who of old

Creative o'er the waters moved:
 Thenceforth the Church, made One and Whole,
Arose in Him, and lived, and loved;
 His Temple she, and He her Soul.

Feast of the Most Holy Trinity

Fall back, all worlds, into the abyss
 That man may contemplate once more
That which He ever was who is;
 The Eternal Essence we adore.

Angelic hierarchies! recede
 Beyond extinct Creation's shade —
What were ye at the first? Decreed:
 Decreed, not fashioned! thought, not made!

Like wind the untold Millenniums passed:
 Sole-throned He sat; yet not alone:
Godhead in Godhead still was glassed;
 The Spirit was breathed from Sire and Son.

Prime Virgin, separate and sealed;
 Nor less of social Love the root!
Dimly in lowliest shapes revealed;
 Entire in every Attribute:

Thou liv'st in all things and around;
 To Thee external is there nought;
Thou of the boundless art the bound;
 And still Creation is Thy Thought.

In vain, O God, our wings we spread;
 So distant are Thou — yet so nigh.
Remains but this when all is said
 For Thee to live; in Thee to die.

The Croppy Boy
A Ballad of '98

'Good men and true! in this house who dwell,
To a stranger *bouchal*, I pray you tell
Is the Priest at home? or may he be seen?
I would speak a word with Father Green.'

'The Priest's at home, boy, and may be seen;
'Tis easy speaking with Father Green;
But you must wait, till I go and see
If the holy Father alone may be.'

The youth has entered an empty hall —
What a lonely sound has his light foot-fall!
And the gloomy chamber's chill and bare,
With a vested Priest in a lonely chair.

The youth has knelt to tell his sins,
'*Nomine Dei*,' the youth begins:
At '*mea culpa*' he beats his breast,
And in broken murmurs he speaks the rest.

'At the siege of Ross did my father fall,
And at Gorey my loving brothers all.
I alone am left of my name and race;
I will go to Wexford and take their place.

'I cursed three times since last Easter Day —
At Mass-time once I went to play;
I passed the churchyard one day in haste,
And forgot to pray for my mother's rest.

bouchal: boy

'I bear no hate against living thing;
But I love my country above my King.
Now, Father! bless me, and let me go
To die, if God has ordained it so.'

The Priest said nought, but a rustling noise
Made the youth look above in wild surprise;
The robes were off, and in scarlet there
Sat a yeoman captain with fiery glare.

With fiery glare and with fury hoarse,
Instead of blessing, he breathed a curse:
"'Twas a good thought, boy, to come here and shrive;
For one short hour is your time to live.

'Upon yon river three tenders float;
The Priest's in one, if he isn't shot;
We hold his house for our Lord the King,
And — "Amen", say I — may all traitors swing!'

At Geneva barrack that young man died,
And at Passage they have his body laid.
Good people who live in peace and joy,
Breathe a prayer and a tear for the Croppy boy.

DENIS FLORENCE MacCARTHY
(1817-1882)

The Paschal Fire

On Tara's hill the daylight dies —
    On Tara's plain 'tis dead;
"Till Baal's unkindled fires shall rise,
    No fire must flame instead.'
'Tis thus the king commanding speaks,
    Commands and speaks in vain —
For lo! a fire defiant breaks,
    From out the woods of Slane.

For there in prayer is Patrick bent,
    With Christ his soul is knit,
And there before his simple tent
    The Paschal fire is lit.
'What means this flame that through the night
    Illumines all the vale?
What rebel hand a fire dare light
    Before the fires of Baal?'

O king! when Baal's dark reign is o'er,
    When thou thyself art gone;
This fire will light the Irish shore,
    And lead its people on:
Will lead them on full many a night
    Through which they're doomed to go,
Like that which led the Israelite
    From bondage and from woe.

This fire, this sacred fire of God,
    Young hearts shall bear afar
To lands no human foot hath trod,
    Beneath the western star.
To lands where Faith's bright flag, unfurled
    By those who here have knelt,
Shall give unto a newer world
    The sceptre of the Celt.

And thus 'twill be, that there and here,
 In hovel or in hall,
One night in each revolving year
 This memory shall recall.
One hour of brightness in their night,
 Where'er the Gael may roam,
When love this festal fire shall light
 For Patrick and for Home!

The Voyage
From *The Voyage of St Brendan*

At length the long-expected morning came,
 When from the opening arms of that wild bay,
Beneath the hill that bears my humble name,
 Over the waves we took our untracked way;
Sweetly the morning lay on tarn and rill,
 Gladly the waves played in its golden light,
And the proud top of the majestic hill
 Shone in the azure air, serene and bright.

Our little bark, kissing the dimpled smiles
 On ocean's cheek, flew like a wanton bird,
And then the land, with all its hundred isles,
 Faded away, and yet we spoke no word.
Each silent tongue held converse with the past,
 Each moistened eye looked round the circling wave,
And, save the spot where stood our trembling mast,
 Saw all things hid within one mighty grave.

We were alone on the wide watery waste —
 Nought broke its bright monotony of blue,
Save where the breeze the flying billows chased,
 Or where the clouds their purple shadows threw.
We were alone — the pilgrims of the sea —
 One boundless azure desert round us spread;
No hope, no trust, no strength, except in THEE,
 Father, who once the pilgrim-peoples led.

And when the bright-faced sun resigned his throne
    Unto the Ethiop queen, who rules the night,
Who, with her pearly crown and starry zone,
    Fills the dark dome of heaven with silvery light; —
As on we sailed, beneath her milder sway,
    And felt within our hearts her holier power,
We ceased from toil, and humbly knelt to pray,
    And hailed with vesper hymns the tranquil hour!

We breathed aloud the Christian's filial prayer,
    Which makes us brothers even with the Lord;
Our Father, cried we, in the midnight air,
    In heaven and earth be thy great name adored;
May thy bright kingdom, where the angels are,
    Replace this fleeting world, so dark and dim.
And then, with eyes fixed on some glorious star,
    We sang the Virgin-Mother's vesper hymn!

Hail, brightest star, that o'er life's troubled sea
    Shines pitying down from heaven's elysian blue!
Mother and Maid, we fondly look to thee,
    Fair gate of bliss, where heaven beams brightly through.
Star of the morning! guide our youthful days,
    Shine on our infant steps in life's long race,
Star of the evening! with thy tranquil rays,
    Gladden the aged eyes that seek thy face.

'Twas thus, in hymns, and prayers, and holy psalms,
    Day tracking day, and night succeeding night,
Now driven by tempests, now delayed by calms,
    Along the sea we winged our varied flight.
Oh! how we longed and pined for sight of land!
    Oh! how we sighed for the green pleasant fields!
Compared with the cold waves, the barest strand —
    The bleakest rock — a crop of comfort yields.

The Pillar Towers of Ireland

The pillar towers of Ireland, how wondrously they stand
By the lakes and rushing rivers through the valleys of our land;
In mystic file, through the isle, they lift their heads sublime,
These grey old pillar temples — these conquerors of time!

Two favourites hath Time — the pyramids of Nile,
And the old mystic temples of our own dear isle;
As the breeze o'er the seas, where the halcyon has its nest,
Thus time o'er Egypt's tombs and the temples of the West!

The names of their founders have vanished in the gloom,
Like the dry branch in the fire or the body in the tomb;
But today, in the ray, their shadows still they cast —
These temples of forgotten gods — these relics of the past!

Around these walls have wandered the Briton and the Dane —
The captives of Armorica, the cavaliers of Spain —
Phoenician and Milesian, and the plundering Norman Peers —
And the swordsmen of brave Brian, and the chiefs of later years!

How many different rites have these grey old temples known?
To the mind what dreams are written in these chronicles of stone!
What terror and what error, what gleams of love and truth,
Have flashed from these walls since the world was in its youth?

Here blazed the sacred fire, and when the sun was gone,
As a star from afar to the traveller it shone;
And the warm blood of the victim have these grey old temples drunk,
And the death-song of the Druid and the matin of the Monk.

Here was placed the holy chalice that held the sacred wine,
And the gold cross from the altar, and the relics from the shrine,
And the mitre shining brighter with its diamonds than the East,
And the crozier of the Pontiff, and the vestements of the Priest!

Where blazed the sacred fire, rang out the vesper bell, —
Where the fugitive found shelter, became the hermit's cell;
And hope hung out its symbol to the innocent and good,
For the Cross o'er the moss of the pointed summit stood!

There may it stand for ever, while this symbol doth impart
To the mind one glorious vision, or one proud throb to the heart;
While the breast needeth rest may these grey old temples last,
Bright prophets of the future, as preachers of the past!

MICHAEL J. BARRY
(1817-1889)

Hymn of Freedom

God of peace! before thee,
   Peaceful, here we kneel,
Humbly to implore thee
   For a nation's weal.
Calm her sons' dissensions,
   Bid their discord cease,
End their mad contentions —
   Hear us, God of Peace!

God of love, low bending,
   To thy throne we turn;
Let thy rays, descending,
   Through our island burn.
Let no strife divide us,
   But, from heaven above,
Look on us and guide us —
   Hear us, God of Love!

God of Battles! aid us:
   Let no despot's might
Trample or degrade us,
   Seeking this our right!
Arm us for the danger;
   Keep all craven fear
To our breasts a stranger —
   God of Battles! hear.

God of Right! preserve us
   Just — as we are strong;
Let no passion swerve us
   To one act of wrong;
Let no thought unholy
   Come our cause to blight;
Thus we pray thee, lowly —
   Hear us, God of Right!

God of Vengeance! smite us
 With thy shaft sublime,
If one bond unite us
 Forged in fraud or crime!
But if, humbly kneeling,
We implore thine ear,
For our rights appealing —
 God of Nations! hear.

EMILY BRONTË
(1818-1848)

No Coward Soul

No coward soul is mine,
No trembler in the world's storm-troubled sphere:
I see Heaven's glories shine,
And Faith shines equal, arming me from Fear.

O God within my breast,
Almighty, ever-present Deity!
Life, that in me has rest
As I, undying Life, have power in thee!

Vain are the thousand creeds
That move men's hearts, unutterably vain;
Worthless as withered weeds,
Or idlest froth amid the boundless main,

To wake doubt in one,
Holding so fast by thy infinity,
So surely anchored on
The steadfast rock of Immortality.

With wide-embracing love
Thy Spirit animates eternal years,
Pervades and broods above,
Changes, sustains, dissolves, creates and rears.

Though earth and man were gone,
And suns and universes ceased to be,
And Thou were left alone,
Every Existence would exist in Thee.

There is not room for Death,
Nor atom that His might could render void:
Since Thou art Being and Breath,
And what Thou art may never be destroyed.

FRANCES ALEXANDER
(1818-1895)

All Things Bright and Beautiful

All things bright and beautiful,
    All creatures great and small,
All things wise and wonderful,
    The Lord God made them all.

Each little flower that opens,
    Each little bird that sings,
He made their glowing colours,
    He made their tiny wings.

The purple-headed mountain,
    The river running by,
The sunset, and the morning,
    That brightens up the sky;

The cold wind in the winter,
    The pleasant summer sun,
The ripe fruits in the garden,
    He made them every one.

He gave us eyes to see them,
    And lips that we might tell,
How great is God Almighty,
    Who has made all things well.

There is a Green Hill far away

There is a green hill far away,
    Without a city wall,
Where the dear Lord was crucified,
    Who died to save us all.

We may not know, we cannot tell
　　What pains He had to bear,
But we believe it was for us
　　He hung and suffered there.

He died that we might be forgiven,
　　He died to make us good,
That we might go at last to heaven,
　　Saved by His precious blood.

There was no other good enough
　　To pay the price of sin,
He only could unlock the gate
　　Of heaven, and let us in.

His are the Thousand Sparkling Rills

His are the thousand sparkling rills
　　That from a thousand fountains burst,
And fill with music all the hills;
　　And yet He saith, 'I thirst.'

All fiery pangs on battle-fields,
　　On fever beds where sick men toss,
Are in that human cry He yields
　　To anguish on the cross.

But more than pains that racked Him then
　　Was the deep longing thirst Divine
That thirsted for the souls of men:
　　Dear Lord! and one was mine.

O Love most patient, give me grace;
　　Make all my soul athirst for Thee;
That parched dry Lip, that fading Face,
　　That Thirst were all for me.

LADY WILDE
(SPERANZA)
(1820-1896)

The Famine Year

Weary men, what reap ye? — 'Golden corn for the stranger.'
What sow ye? — 'Human corses that wait for the avenger.'
Fainting forms, hunger-stricken, what see ye in the offing?
'Stately ships to bear our food away amid the stranger's scoffing.'
There's a proud array of soldiers — what do they round your door?
'They guard our master's granaries from the thin hands of the poor.'
Pale mothers, wherefore weeping? — 'Would to God that we were
      dead —
Our children swoon before us, and we cannot give them bread!'

Little children, tears are strange upon your infant faces,
God meant you but to smile within your mother's soft embraces.
'Oh! we know not what is smiling, and we know not what is dying;
But we're hungry, very hungry, and we cannot stop our crying.
And some of us grow cold and white — we know not what it means;
But as they lie beside us we tremble in our dreams.'
There's a gaunt crowd on the highway — are you come to pray to man,
With hollow eyes that cannot weep, and for words your faces wan?

'No; the blood is dead within our veins — we care not now for life;
Let us die hid in the ditches, far from children and from wife!
We cannot stay to listen to their raving famished cries —
Bread! Bread! Bread! and none to still their agonies.
We left an infant playing with her dead mother's hand:
We left a maiden maddened by the fever's scorching brand:'
Better, maiden, thou wert strangled in thy own dark-twisted tresses!
Better, infant, thou wert smothered in thy mother's first caresses.

'We are fainting in our misery, but God will hear our groan;
Yet, if fellow-men desert us, will He harken from His throne?
Accursed are we in our own land, yet toil we still and toil;
But the stranger reaps our harvest — the alien owns our soil.
O Christ! how have we sinned, that on our native plains

We perish homeless, naked, starved, with branded brow like Cain's?
Dying, dying wearily, with a torture sure and slow —
Dying as a dog would die, by the wayside as we go.

'One by one they're falling round us, their pale faces to the sky;
We've no strength left to dig them graves — there let them lie.
The wild bird, if he's stricken, is mourned by the others,
But we — we die in Christian land, — we die amid our brothers,
In the land which God has given, like a wild beast in his cave,
Without a tear, a prayer, a shroud, a coffin, or a grave.
Ha! but think ye the contortions on each livid face we see,
Will not be read on Judgment-day by eyes of Deity?

'We are wretches, famished, scorned, human tools to build your pride,
But God will yet take vengeance for the souls for whom Christ died.
Now is your hour of pleasure — bask ye in the world's caress;
But our whitening bones against ye will rise as witnesses,
From the cabins and the ditches in their charred, uncoffined masses,
For the Angel of the Trumpet will know them as he passes.
A ghastly spectral army, before great God we'll stand,
And arraign ye as our murderers, O spoilers of our land!'

WILLIAM ALLINGHAM
(1824-1889)

The Girl's Lamentation

With grief and mourning I sit to spin;
My love passed by, and he didn't come in;
My love passed by, and he didn't come in;
He passes by me both day and night,
And carries off my poor heart's delight.

Says he, 'We'll wed without loss of time,
And sure our love's but a little crime.'
My apron-string now it's wearing short,
And my love he seeks other girls to court.

O with him I'd go if I had my will,
I'd follow him barefoot o'er rock and hill;
I'd never once speak of all my grief
If he'd give me a smile for my heart's relief.

In our wee garden the rose unfolds,
With bachelor's-buttons and marigolds;
I'll tie no posies for dance or fair,
A willow-twig is for me to wear.

For a maid again I can never be,
Till the red rose blooms on the willow tree.
Of such a trouble I've heard them tell,
And now I know what it means full well.

As through the long lonesome night I lie,
I'd give the world if I might but cry;
But I mus'n't moan there or raise my voice,
And the tears run down without any noise.

And what, O what will my mother say?
She'll wish her daughter was in the clay.
My father will curse me to my face;
The neighbours will know of my black disgrace.

The Candlemas crosses hang near my bed;
To look at them puts me much in dread,
They mark the good time that's gone and past:
It's like this year's one will prove the last.

The oldest cross it's a dusty brown,
But the winter winds didn't shake it down;
The newest cross keeps the colour bright;
When the straw was reaping my heart was light.

When the straw was weaving my heart was glad,
For neither sin nor shame I had,
In the barn where oat-chaff was flying round,
And the thumping flails made a pleasant sound.

Now summer or winter to me it's one;
But Oh! for a day like the time that's gone!
I'd little care was it storm or shine,
If I had but peace in this heart of mine.

Oh! light and false is a young man's kiss,
And a foolish girl gives her soul for this.
Oh! light and short is the young man's blame,
And a helpless girl has the grief and shame.

To the river-bank once I thought to go,
And cast myself in the stream below;
I thought 'twould carry us far out to sea,
Where they'd never find my poor babe and me.

Sweet Lord, forgive me that wicked mind!
You know I used to be well inclined.
Oh, take compassion upon my state,
Because my trouble is so very great.

My head turns round with the spinning-wheel,
And a heavy cloud on my eyes I feel.
But the worst of all is at my heart's core;
For my innocent days will come back no more.

The Abbot of Inisfalen

I

The Abbot of Inisfalen
    Awoke ere dawn of day;
Under the dewy green leaves
    Went he forth to pray.

The lake around his island
    Lay smooth and dark and deep,
And wrapt in a misty stillness
    The mountains were all asleep.

Low kneeled the Abbot Cormac,
    When the dawn was dim and grey;
The prayers of his holy office
    He faithfully 'gan say.

Low kneel'd the Abbot Cormac,
    When the dawn was waxing red;
And for his sins' forgiveness
    A solemn prayer he said.

Low kneel'd that blessed Abbot
    When the dawn was waxing bright;
He pray'd a great prayer for Ireland,
    He pray'd with all his might.

Low kneel'd that good old Father,
    When the sun began to dart;
He pray'd a prayer for all mankind,
    He pray'd it from his heart.

II

The Abbot of Inisfalen
    Arose upon his feet;
He heard a small bird singing,
    And O but it sung sweet!

He heard a white bird singing well
 Within a holly-tree;
A song so sweet and happy
 Never before heard he.

It sung upon a hazel,
 It sung upon a thorn;
He had never heard such music
 Since the hour that he was born.

Till at last he well bethought him,
 He might no longer stay;
So he blessed the little white singing bird,
 And gladly went his way.

III

But, when he came to his Abbey walls,
 He found a wondrous change;
He saw no friendly faces there,
 For every face was strange.

The strange men spoke unto him;
 And he heard from all and each
The foreign tongue of the Sassenach,
 Not wholesome Irish speech.

Then the oldest monk came forward,
 In Irish tongue spake he:
'Thou wearest the holy Augustine's dress,
 And who hath given it to thee?'

'I wear the holy Augustine's dress,
 And Cormac is my name,
The Abbot of this good Abbey
 By grace of God I am.

'I went forth to pray, at the dawn of day,
 And when my prayers were said,
I hearken'd awhile to a little bird,
 That sung above my head.'

The monk to him made answer,
    'Two hundred years have gone o'er,
Since our Abbot Cormac went through the gate,
    And never was heard of more.

'Matthias now is our Abbot,
    And twenty have passs'd away;
The stranger is lord of Ireland;
    We live in an evil day.'

IV

'Now give me absolution;
    For my time is come,' said he.
And they gave him absolution,
    As speedily as might be.

Then, close outside the window,
    The sweetest song they heard
That ever yet since the world began
    Was utter'd by any bird.

The monks look'd out and saw the bird,
    Its feathers all white and clean;
And there in a moment, beside it,
    Another white bird was seen.

Those two they sang together,
    Waved their white wings and fled:
Flew aloft, and vanish'd;
    But the good old man was dead.

They buried his blessed body
    Where lake and greensward meet;
A carven cross above his head,
    A holly-bush at his feet;

Where spreads the beautiful water
    To gay or cloudy skies,
And the purple peaks of Killarney
    From ancient woods arise.

THOMAS D'ARCY MAGEE
(1825-1868)

The Celts

Long, long ago, beyond the misty space
    Of twice a thousand years,
In Erin old there dwelt a mighty race,
    Taller than Roman spears;
Like oaks and towers they had a giant grace,
    Were fleet as deers,
With wind and waves they made their 'biding place,
    These western, shepherd seers.

Their Ocean-God was Manannan, MacLir,
    Whose angry lips,
In their white foam, full often would inter
    Whole fleets of ships;
Cromah their Day-God, and their Thunderer
    Made morning and eclipse;
Bride was their Queen of Song, and unto her
    They prayed with fire-touched lips.

Great were their deeds, their passions and their sports;
    With clay and stone
They piled on strath and shore those mystic forts,
    Not yet o'erthrown;
On cairn-crowned hills they held their council-courts;
    While youths alone,
With giant dogs, explored the elk resorts,
    And brought them down.

Of these was Fin, the father of the Bard
    Whose ancient song
Over the clamour of all change is heard,
    Sweet-voiced and strong.
Fin once o'ertook Grania, the golden-haired,
    The fleet and young;
From her the lovely, and from him the feared,
    The primal poet sprung.

Ossian! two thousand years of mist and change
    Surround thy name —
Thy Fenian heroes now no longer range
    The hills of fame.
The very names of Fin and Gaul sound strange —
    Yet thine the same —
By miscalled lake and desecrated grange —
    Remains, and shall remain!

The Celtic Cross

Through storm and fire and gloom, I see it stand
    Firm, broad, and tall,
The Celtic Cross that marks our Fatherland,
    Amid them all!
Druids and Danes and Saxons vainly rage
    Around its base;
It standeth shock on shock, and age on age,
    Star of our scatter'd race.

O Holy Cross! dear symbol of the dread
    Death of our Lord,
Around thee long have slept our martyr dead
    Sward over sward.
And hundred bishops I myself can count
    Among the slain:
Chiefs, captains, rank and file, a shining mount
    Of God's ripe grain.

The monarch's mace, the Puritan's claymore,
    Smote thee not down;
On headland steep, on mountain summit hoar,
    In mart and town,
In Glendalough, in Ara, in Tyrone,
    We find thee still,
Thy open arms still stretched to thine own,
    O'er town and lough and hill.

And would they tear thee out of Irish soil,
    The guilty fools!
How time must mock their antiquated toil
    And broken tools!
Cranmer and Cromwell from thy grasp retired,
    Baffled and thrown;
William and Anne to sap thy site conspir'd —
    The rest is known.

Holy Patrick, father of our faith,
    Beloved of God!
Shield thy dear Church from impending scaith,
    Or, if the rod
Must scourge it yet again, inspire and raise
    To emprise high
Men like the heroic race of other days,
    Who joyed to die.

Fear! wherefore should the Celtic people fear
    Their Church's fate?
The day is not — the day was never near —
    Could desolate
The Destined Island, all whose clay
    Is holy ground:
Its Cross shall stand till that predestin'd day
    When Erin's self is drowned.

ARTHUR O'SHAUGHNESSY
(1844-1881)

The Line of Beauty

When mountains crumble and rivers all run dry,
    When every flower has fallen and summer fails
    To come again, when the sun's splendour pales,
And earth with lagging footsteps seems well-nigh
Spent in her annual circuit through the sky;
    When love is a quenched flame, and nought avails
    To save decrepit man, who feebly wails
And lies down lost in the great grave to die;
What is eternal? What escapes decay?
    A certain faultless, matchless, deathless line,
    Curving consummate. Death, Eternity,
And nought to it, from it take nought away:
    'Twas all God's gift and all man's mastery,
    God become human and man grown divine.

The Infinite

The Infinite always is silent:
It is only the Finite speaks —
Our words are the idle wave-caps
On the deep that never breaks.
We may question with word of science,
Explain, decide and discuss;
But only in meditation
The Mystery speaks to us.

The Lure

'What bait do you use,' said a Saint to the Devil,
'When you fish where the souls of men abound?'
'Well, for special tastes,' said the King of Evil,
'Gold and Fame are the best I've found.'
'But for common use?' asked the Saint. 'Ah then,'
Said the Demon, 'I angle for Man, not men,
          And a thing I hate
          Is to change my bait,
So I fish with a woman the whole year round'.

OSCAR WILDE
(1854-1900)

From *The Ballad of Reading Gaol*

There is no chapel on the day
    On which they hang a man:
The Chaplain's heart is far too sick,
    Or his face is far too wan,
Or there is that written in his eyes
    Which none should look upon.

So they kept us close till nigh on noon,
    And then they rang the bell,
And the Warders with their jingling keys
    Opened each listening cell,
And down the iron stairs we tramped,
    Each from his separate Hell.

Out into God's sweet air we went,
    But not in wonted way,
For this man's face was white with fear,
    And that man's face was grey,
And I never saw sad men who looked
    So wistfully at the day.

I never saw sad men who looked
    With such a wistful eye
Upon that little tent of blue
    We prisoners called the sky,
And at every careless cloud that passed
    In happy freedom by . . .

Silently we went round and round,
    And through each hollow mind
The Memory of dreadful things
    Rushed like a dreadful wind,
And Horror stalked before each man,
    And Terror crept behind . . .

With midnight always in one's heart,
      And twilight in one's cell,
We turn the crank, or tear the rope,
      Each in his separate Hell,
And the silence is more awful far
      Than the sound of a brazen bell.

And never a human voice comes near
      To speak a gentle word:
And the eye that watches through the door
      Is pitiless and hard:
And by all forgot, we rot and rot,
      With soul and body marred.

And thus we rust Life's iron chain
      Degraded and alone:
And some men curse and some men weep,
      And some men make no moan:
But God's Eternal Laws are kind
      And break the heart of stone.

And every human heart that breaks
      In prison-cell or yard,
Is as that broken box that gave
      Its treasure to the Lord,
And filled the unclean leper's house
      With the scent of costliest nard.

Ah! happy they whose hearts can break
      And peace of pardon win!
How else may man make straight his plan
      And cleanse his soul from Sin?
How else but through a broken heart
      May Lord Christ enter in?

And he of the swollen purple throat
      And the stark and staring eyes,
Waits for the holy hands that took
      The Thief to Paradise;
And a broken and a contrite heart
      The Lord will not despise . . .

In Reading gaol by Reading town
    There is a pit of shame,
And in it lies a wretched man
    Eaten by teeth of flame,
In a burning winding-sheet he lies,
    And his grave has got no name.

And there, till Christ call forth the dead,
    In silence let him lie:
No need to waste the foolish tear,
    Or heave the windy sigh:
The man had killed the thing he loved,
    And so he had to die.

And all men kill the thing they love,
    By all let this be heard,
Some do it with a bitter look,
    Some with a flattering word,
The coward does it with a kiss,
    The brave man with a sword!

E Tenebris

Come down, O Christ, and help me! reach Thy hand,
    For I am drowning in a stormier sea
    Than Simon on Thy Lake of Galilee:
The wine of life is spilt upon the sand,
My heart is as some famine-murdered land
    Whence all good things have perished utterly,
    And well I know my soul in Hell must lie
If I this night before God's throne should stand.
'He sleeps perchance, or rideth to the chase,
    Like Baal, when his prophets howled that name
        From morn to noon on Carmel's smitten height.'
Nay, peace, I shall behold, before the night,
    The feet of brass, the robe more white than flame,
The wounded hands, the weary human face.

San Miniato

See, I have climbed the mountain side
Up to this holy house of God,
Where once that Angel-Painter trod
Who saw the heavens open wide,

And throned upon the crescent moon
The Virginal white Queen of Grace —
Mary! could I but see thy face
Death could not come at all too soon.

O crowned by God with thorns and pain!
Mother of Christ! O mystic wife!
My heart is weary of this life
And over-sad to sing again.

O crowned by God with love and flame!
O crowned by Christ the Holy One!
O listen ere the searching sun
Show to the world my sin and shame.

Hélas

To drift with every passion till my soul
Is a stringed lute on which all winds can play,
Is it for this that I have given away
Mine ancient wisdom, and austere control?
Methinks my life is a twice-written scroll
Scrawled over on some boyish holiday
With idle songs for pipe and virelay,
Which do but mar the secret of the whole.
Surely there was a time I might have trod
The sunlit heights, and from life's dissonance
Struck one clear chord to reach the ears of God:
Is that time dead? lo! with a little rod
I did but touch the honey of romance —
And must I lose a soul's inheritance?

KATHERINE TYNAN
(1861-1931)

Mater Dei

She looked to east, she looked to west,
  Her eyes unfathomable, mild,
That saw both worlds, came home to rest —
  Home to her own sweet child.
  God's golden head was at her breast.

What need to look o'er land and sea?
  What could the winged ships being to her?
What gold or gems of price might be,
  Ivory or miniver,
Since God Himself lay on her knee?

What could th' intense blue heaven keep
  To draw her eyes and thoughts so high?
All heaven was where her Boy did leap,
  Where her foot quietly
Went rocking the dear God asleep.

The angel folk fared up and down
  A Jacob's Ladder hung between
Her quiet chamber and God's Town.
  She saw unawed, serene;
Since God Himself played by her gown.

The Man of the House

Joseph, honoured from Sea to Sea,
This is your name that pleases me,
  'Man of the House.'

I see you rise at the dawn and light
The fire and blow till the flame is bright.

I see you take the pitcher and carry
The deep well-water for Jesus and Mary.

You knead the corn for the bread so fine,
Gather them grapes from the hanging vine.

There are little feet that are soft and slow,
Follow you whithersoever you go.

There's a little face at your workshop door,
A little one sits down on your floor.

Holds His hands for the shavings curled,
The soft little hands that have made the world.

Mary calls you: the meal is ready;
You swing the Child to your shoulder steady.

I see your quiet smile as you sit
And watch the little Son thrive and eat.

The vine curls by the window space,
The wings of angels cover the face.

Up in the rafters, polished and olden,
There's a Dove that broods and his wings are golden.

You who kept them through shine and storm,
A staff, a shelter kindly and warm.

Father of Jesus, husband of Mary,
Hold up your lilies for Sanctuary!

Joseph, honoured from Sea to Sea,
Guard me and mine and my own rooftree.
      'Man of the House!'

The Making of Birds

God made Him birds in a pleasant humour;
　　Tired of planets and suns was He.
He said: 'I will add a glory to summer,
　　Gifts for my creatures banished from Me!'

He had a thought and it set Him smiling
　　Of the shape of a bird and its glancing head,
Its dainty air and its grace beguiling:
　　'I will make feathers,' the Lord God said.

He made the robin; He made the swallow:
　　His deft hands moulding the shape to His mood,
The thrush and the lark and the finch to follow,
　　And laughed to see that His work was good.

He Who has given men gift of laughter,
　　Made in His image; He fashioned fit
The blink of the owl and the stork thereafter,
　　The little wren and the long-tailed tit.

He spent in making His wit and fancies;
　　The wing-feathers He fashioned them strong;
Deft and dear as daisies and pansies,
　　He crowned His work with the gift of song.

'Dearlings,' He said, 'make songs for My praises!'
　　He tossed them loose to the sun and wind,
Airily sweet as pansies and daisies;
　　He taught them to build a nest to their mind.

The dear Lord God of His glories weary —
　　Christ our Lord had the heart of a boy —
Made Him birds in a moment merry,
　　Bade them soar and sing for His joy.

Sheep and Lambs

All in the April evening,
    April airs were abroad;
The sheep with their little lambs
    Passed me by on the road.

The sheep with their little lambs
    Passed me by on the road;
All in an April evening
    I thought on the Lamb of God.

The lambs were weary, and crying
    With a weak human cry.
I thought on the Lamb of God
    Going meekly to die.

Up in the blue, blue mountains
    Dewy pastures are sweet;
Rest for the little bodies,
    Rest for the little feet.

But for the Lamb of God
    Up on the hill-top green,
Only a cross of shame
    Two stark crosses between.

All in the April evening,
    April airs were abroad;
I saw the sheep and their lambs,
    And thought on the Lamb of God.

Holy Family

Thy kingdom come: yea, bid it come —
    But, when thy kingdom first began
On earth, thy kingdom was a home,
    A child, a woman, and a man.

The child was in the midst thereof,
　　O blessed Jesus, holiest One!
The centre and the fount of love,
　　Mary and Joseph's little Son.

Wherever on this earth shall be
　　A child, a woman and a man,
Imaging that sweet trinity
　　Wherewith thy kingdom first began,

Establish there thy kingdom! Yea,
　　And o'er that trinity of love
Send down, as in thy appointed day,
　　The brooding spirit of thy Dove!

SIR ROGER CASEMENT
(1864-1916)

Lost Youth

Weep not that you no longer feel the tide
    High breasting sun and storm that bore along
    Your youth in currents of perpetual song;
For in these mid-sea waters, still and wide,
A sleepless purpose the great deep doth hide.
    Here spring the mighty fountains, pure and strong,
    That bear sweet change of breath to city throng,
Who, had the sea no breeze, would soon have died.

So, though the sun shines not in such a blue,
    Nor have the stars the meaning youth devised,
The heavens are nigher, and a light shines through —
    The brightness that not sun nor stars sufficed;
And on this lonely waste we find it true
    Lost youth and love not lost, are hid with Christ.

Fragment
Thoughts suggested by a stern friend's character

He is an inharmonious note,
He represents the victor and the strong;
Kind-hearted, yet with such a sense of right
There is no sorrow in him for the wrong:
No pity for its doers; he would smite
All evil men, and Mercy finds no place
On that stern brow one pitying line to trace.
These are the eyes, and such strong brows are these
Have fronted England's foes on hundred seas.
O! thou wast once a little child, whom night
And puppy dogs, and even birds could fright —
A weak child dangled on weak woman's knees.
Thou wast not always strong thyself — and these
Who now earn nought but scorn, because more weak

Than thou, they turn from bitter truth, and seek
With Pleasure's roses dallying to recall
That man was born to love — if born to fall!
They claim our love, they need our stronger grasp
Sin's brows of shame, rose-hidden to unmask.

For there *is* beauty in the devious path
That turns from too stern duty, and the wrath
That only knows to punish, and goes in
As to its proper goal, the haunts of sin;
Not ever stern, with cold, repellent eye
To mark the evil man, and pass him by;
But with a gentle hand direct him right,
Turn not the wrong, but his good deed to light.
The sternly righteous heart one day will fare
To its own doom; the pity He finds there
May be the measure of God's mercy too.

Are we more pure than Christ who loved and knew
Vile sinners, fed with them, and never scorned
One sinful hand, tho' its misdeeds he mourned;
He kept His anger for that rigid school
Who measure Virtue, like a gown, by rule —
Who wear their righteousness as Sunday clothes,
That would be soiled by meaner people's woes;
His healing robe the leper's hand might pull.
God! break my heart — but make it pitiful!

Forest Thoughts

But oh! how different is each sight and sound
    When in the east the golden morn appears
And the wood's depths to life wake with a bound
    As from her robe she shakes night's dreary tears.

And as upswells the breeze's rising strife,
    Amid the still leaves with a rustling sound —
How sweet to hear the sounds of wakening life
    Rise from each bush and fragrant copse around.

From moved bough, the thrush, or near its nest,
    Pours forth its anthem to the brightening morn —
With parted bill, and swelling throat and breast
    Rejoicing that another day is born.

And overhead I hear the piping call
    Of blackbird to its mate in soft delight —
Then breaking from the trees the rushing fall
    Of the wood pigeon's wings in startled flight.

Now rabbits too begin to dot the scene
    And frisk and scamper on some open glade —
To crop the wild thyme and the grasses green
    While squirrels' bright eyes peep from out the shade.

Yet sad to think while hymns from woods and fields
    On morning's earliest breath to God are borne,
That man alone of all creation yields
    No thanks to Him to meet another morn.

Yes, man who ranks himself as next of kin
    To heaven's angels, and is linked to God
By bonds of filial love, sees day begin
    Breathing less praise than breathes the dewy sod!

Thankless he wakes; no song begins his day;
    His wearied thoughts renew their old unrest;
Both 'neath a sullen cloud pursue their way
    'Till night, not darker, folds them to its breast.

Days are the bricks that build the hours of Life,
    And illspent days like bricks unfirmly laid
But raise a structure which in man's mid strife
    May fall a ruin he himself has made.

Prize then the morn, 'tis childhood of the day
    And as we train the child to make the man —
So spend the morning that each heart can say
    'I fear not for the hours such work began.'

Wake not to morn then with a sullen heart
    But with a thankful prayer that God has given
Another day on which anew to start
    Upon the path of life which leads to Heaven.

STEPHEN LUCIUS GWYNN
(1864-1950)

On One Dying in a Convent

Here where the meadows gave ease to tired feet,
Far from all haste and rattle of the street,
Here where the convent-life, ordered for prayer,
Quickened and purged and sanctified the air —
While a war raved and threatened, she found peace,
Till in pure gentleness, God gave release.
Tranquilly sleeping, she passed beyond strife,
Borne out on the broad ebb of tidal life.
Here let the form we knew melt in the sod;
What was her spirit, has sunk back to God.

WILLIAM BUTLER YEATS
(1865-1939)

Sailing to Byzantium

That is no country for old men. The young
In one another's arms, birds in the trees
— Those dying generations — at their song,
The salmon-falls, the mackerel-crowded seas,
Fish, flesh, or fowl, commend all summer long
Whatever is begotten, born and dies.
Caught in that sensual music all neglect
Monuments of unageing intellect.

An aged man is but a paltry thing,
A tattered coat upon a stick, unless
Soul clap its hands and sing, and louder sing
For every tatter in its mortal dress,
Nor is there singing school but studying
Monuments of its own magnificence;
And therefore I have sailed the seas and come
To the holy city of Byzantium.

O sages standing in God's holy fire
As in the gold mosaic of a wall,
Come from the holy fire, perne in a gyre,
And be the singing-masters of my soul.
Consume my heart away; sick with desire
And fastened to a dying animal
It knows not what it is; and gather me
Into the artifice of eternity.

Once out of nature I shall never take
My bodily form from any natural thing,
But such a form as Grecian goldsmiths make
Of hammered gold and gold enamelling
To keep a drowsy Emperor awake;
Or set upon a golden bough to sing
To lords and ladies of Byzantium
Of what is past, or passing, or to come.

The Ballad of Father Gilligan

The old priest Peter Gilligan
    Was weary night and day;
For half his flock were in their beds,
    Or under green sods lay.

Once, while he nodded on a chair,
    At the moth-hour of eve,
Another poor man sent for him,
    And he began to grieve.

'I have no rest, nor joy, nor peace,
    For people die and die;'
And after cried he, 'God forgive!
    My body spake, not I!'

He knelt and, leaning on the chair,
    He prayed and fell asleep;
And the moth-hour went from the fields,
    And stars began to peep.

They slowly into millions grew,
    And leaves shook in the wind,
And God covered the world with shade,
    And whispered to mankind.

Upon the time of sparrow chirp
    When the moths came once more,
The old priest Peter Gilligan
    Stood upright on the floor.

'Mavrone, mavrone! the man has died,
While I slept on the chair;'
He roused the horse out of its sleep,
    And rode with little care.

He rode now as he never rode,
    By rocky lane and fen;
The sick man's wife opened the door;
    'Father! you come again!'

'And is the poor man dead?' he cried.
    'He died an hour ago.'
The old priest Peter Gilligan
    In grief swayed to and fro.

'When you were gone, he turned and died
    As merry as a bird.'
The old priest Peter Gilligan
    He knelt him at that word.

'He who hath made the night of stars
    For souls who tire and bleed,
Sent one of His great angels down
    To help me in my need.

'He who is wrapped in purple robes,
    With planets in His care,
Hath pity on the least of things
    Asleep upon a chair.'

A Prayer for My Son

Bid a strong ghost stand at the head
That my Michael may sleep sound,
Nor cry, nor turn in the bed
Till his morning meal come round;
And may departing twilight keep
All dread afar till morning's back,
That his mother may not lack
Her fill of sleep.

Bid the ghost have sword in fist:
Some there are, for I avow
Such devilish things exist,
Who have planned his murder, for they know
Of some most haughty deed or thought
That waits upon his future days,
And would through hatred of the bays
Bring that to nought.

Though You can fashion everything
From nothing every day, and teach
The morning stars to sing,
You have lacked articulate speech
To tell Your simplest want, and known,
Wailing upon a woman's knee,
All of that worst ignominy
Of flesh and bone;

And when through all the town there ran
The servants of Your enemy,
A woman and a man,
Unless the Holy Writings lie,
Hurried through the smooth and rough
And through the fertile and waste,
Protecting, till the danger past,
With human love.

Ireland

'Twas the dream of a God,
     And the mould of His hand,
That you shook 'neath His stroke,
That you trembled and broke
     To this beautiful land.

Here he loosed from His hold
     A brown tumult of wings,
Till the wind on the sea
Bore the strange melody
     Of an island that sings.

He made you all fair,
     You in purple and gold,
You in silver and green,
Till no eye that has seen
     Without love can behold.

I have left you behind
     In the path of the past,
With the white breath of flowers,
With the best of God's hours,
     I have left you at last.

SUSAN L. MITCHELL
(1866-1926)

Immortality

Age cannot reach me where the veils of God
    Have shut me in,
For me the myriad births of stars and suns
    Do but begin,
And here how fragantly there blows to me
    The hóly breath,
Sweet from the flowers and stars and the hearts of men,
    From life and death.

We are not old, O heart, we are not old,
    The breath that blows
The soul aflame is still a wandering wind
    That comes and goes;
And the stirred heart with sudden raptured life
    A moment glows.

A moment here — a bulrush's brown head
    In the grey rain,
A moment there — a child drowned and a heart
    Quickened with pain;
The name of Death, the blue deep heaven, the scent
    Of the salt sea,
The spicy grass, the honey robbed
    From the wild bee.

Awhile we walk the world on its wide roads
    and narrow ways,
And they pass by, the countless shadowy groups
    of nights and days;
We know them not, O happy heart,
    For you and I
Watch where within a slow dawn lightens up
    Another sky.

The Descent of the Child

Who can bring back the magic of that story,
    The singing seraphim, the kneeling kings,
The starry path by which the Child of Glory
    'Mid breathless watchers and through myriad wings
Came, with the heaven behind Him slowly waning,
    Dark with His loss, unto the brightening earth,
The young, ennobled star, that He, so deigning,
    Chose for the heavenly city of His birth?
What but the heart of youth can hold the story,
    The young child's heart, so gentle and so wild,
It can recall the magic of that Glory
    That dreamed itself into a little child.

LIONEL JOHNSON
(1867-1917)

Saint Columba

Dead is Columba: the world's arch
    Gleams with a lightning of strange fires,
They flash and run, they leap and march,
    Signs of a saint's fulfilled desires.

Live is Columba: golden crowned,
    Sceptered with Mary lilies, shod
With angel flames, and girded round
    With white of snow, he goes to God.

No more the grey eyes long to see
    The oakwoods of their Inisfail,
Where the white angels hovering be,
    And ah! the birds in every vale.

No more for him thy fierce winds blow,
    Iona of the angry sea!
Gone, the white glories of they snow,
    And white spray flying over thee!

Now, far from the grey sea, and far
    From the sea-worn rocks and the sea-birds' cries,
Columba hails the morning star
    That shines in never-nighted skies.

High in the perfect Land of Morn,
    He listens to the chaunting air:
The Land where music is not born,
    For music is eternal there.

There, bent before the burning Throne,
    He lauds the lover of the Gael:
Sweet Christ! whom Patrick's children own:
    Glory be thine from Inisfail!

Te Martyrum Candidatus

Ah, see the fair chivalry come, the companions of Christ!
White Horsemen, who ride on white horses, the Knights of God!
They, for their Lord and their Lover who sacrificed
All, save the sweetness of treading, where he first trod!

These, through the darkness of death, the dominion of night,
Swept, and they woke in white places at morning tide:
They saw with their eyes, and sang for joy of the sight,
They saw with their eyes the Eyes of the Crucified.

Now, whithersoever He goeth, with Him they go:
White Horsemen, who ride on white horses, oh, fair to see!
They ride, where the Rivers of Paradise flash and flow,
White Horsemen, with Christ their Captain: for ever He!

GEORGE RUSSELL (A.E.)
(1867-1935)

Immortality

We must pass like smoke or live within the spirit's fire;
For we can no more than smoke unto the flame return
If our thought has changed to dream, our will unto desire,
As smoke we vanish though the fire may burn.

Lights of infinite pity star the grey dusk of our days;
Surely here is soul: with it we have eternal breath:
In the fire of love we live, or pass by many ways,
By unnumbered ways of dream to death.

Prayer

Let us leave our island woods grown dim and blue;
O'er the waters creeping the pearl dust of eve
Hides the silver of the long wave rippling through:
     The chill for the warm room let us leave.

Turn the lamp down low and draw the curtain wide,
So the greyness of the starlight bathes the room;
Let us see the giant face of night outside,
     Though vague as a moth's wing is the gloom.

Rumour of the fierce-pulsed city far away
Breaks upon the peace that aureoles our rest,
Steeped in stillness as if some primeval day
     Hung drowsily o'er the water's breast.

Shut the eyes that flame and hush the heart that burns:
In quiet we may hear the old primeval cry:
God gives wisdom to the spirit that upturns:
     Let us adore now, you and I.

Age on age is heaped about us as we hear:
Cycles hurry to and fro with giant tread
From the deep unto the deep: but do not fear,
For the soul unhearing them is dead.

Desire

With Thee a moment! Then what dreams have play!
Traditions of eternal toil arise,
Search for the high, austere and lonely way
The Spirit moves in through eternities.
Ah, in the soul what memories arise!

And with what yearning inexpressible,
Rising from long forgetfulness I turn
To Thee, invisible, unrumoured, still:
White for Thy whiteness all desires burn.
Ah, with what longing once again I turn!

EVA GORE-BOOTH
(1870-1926)

A Heretic's Pilgrimage

Here, all star-paven at our Lady's well,
A milky way of white anemones
Leads to her simple shrine among the trees,
The silver willow woods of Lissadel.
Grey winds pass sighing and strange forces thrill
The holy water, sheltered from the breeze,
Fresh from the spring of earth's lost mysteries
Beneath the shadow of the haunted hill.
Madonna of the way-side thronèd here!
We bring thee poppies grown amongst the wheat,
Frail blue-bells and the silver marguerite,
And all the golden tribute of the year,
We lay our dreams and flowers at thy feet,
Because the country people hold thee dear.

Above her head full seven cold glories shine,
Before the mighty Virgin Gabriel stands —
His feet are flame, and in his claspèd hands
He holds a tall white lily for a sign.
This is the mortal angels call divine,
The winds of heaven obey her high commands,
Her's is the secret of all times and lands,
The glory of the temple's inmost shrine.
Ah, Mary Mother, thine it was alone
For all the majesty of youth to find
The spirit's glory out of darkness grown,
To leave the soilèd joys of earth behind,
And seek the splendour of the white unknown,
The sacred loneliness of star and wind.

Hail Virgin spirit of the world's desire,
Have pity on us, who, like thee of late
Saw the great angel at life's outer gate,
And paused to greet him with our hearts on fire,
Yet, went away and sold our souls for hire,

And wandered far in the wild ways of fate
And learned the hunger naught can satiate,
And dragged the angel's lily through the mire.
Ah, pray for us, poor children of blind chance,
Who have lost Hope beneath the world's control,
Forgot the glory of the angel's glance,
The dim light of the half-deciphered scroll,
Our one strange glimpse of God's unknown Romance,
Life's salutation to the virgin soul.

MOIRA O'NEILL
(1870-1955)

Grace for Light

When we were little childer we had a quare wee house,
Away up in the heather by the head o' Brabla' burn;
The hares we'd see them scootin', and we'd hear the crowin' grouse
An' when we'd all be in at night ye'd not get room to turn.

The youngest two She'd put to bed, their faces to the wall,
And the lave of us could sit aroun', just anywhere we might;
Herself 'ud take the rush-dip an' light it for us all,
An' '*God be thanked!*' she would say, — '*now we have a light!*'

Then we'd be to quet the laughin' an' pushin' on the floor,
An' think on One who called us to come and be forgiven;
Himself 'ud put his pipe down, an' say the good word more,
'May the Lam o' God lead us all to the Light o' Heaven!'

There's a ween things that used to be an' now has had their day,
The nine glens of Antrim can show ye many a sight;
But not the quare wee house where we lived up Brabla' way,
Nor a child in all the nine Glens that know the grace for light.

LYNN DOYLE
(1873-1961)

An Ulsterman

I do not like the other sort;
They're tricky an' they're sly,
An' couldn't look you in the face
Whenever they pass by.
Still I'll give in that here an' there,
You'll meet a decent man;
I would make an exception, now,
About wee Michael Dan.

But, then, he's from about the doors,
An' lived here all his days,
An' mixin' with us in an' out,
He's fell into our ways.
He pays his debts an' keeps his word
An' does the best he can.
If only all the Papishes
Were like wee Michael Dan!

A better neighbour couldn't be,
He borrows an' he lends;
An' — bar a while about the Twelfth
When him and me's not friends —
He'll never wait until he's asked
To lend a helpin' han'.
There's quite a wheen of Protestants
I'd swop for Michael Dan.

Of course he'd burn me at the stake,
I know that very well;
An' told me one day to my face
I'm not too far from hell.
But when I backed a bill for him
He met it like a man.
There's sparks of Christianity
About wee Michael Dan.

So, while I have my private doubts
About him reachin' heaven,
His feet keeps purty near the pad
On six days out of seven;
An' if it falls within the scope
Of God Almighty's plan
To save a single Papish soul,
I hope it's Michael Dan.

ALICE FURLONG
(1875-1946)

Anonymous. Translation from the Irish

Fragrant the Prayer

Fragrant the prayer
(Breath of the rose in air!)
My child taught me:
The Son of Mary bought me,
The Son of Mary craved me,
The Son of Mary saved me.
Fragrant the prayer,
Breath of the rose in air!

In grey of morn
(Christ was forlorn!)
The birds call kindly:
Be not my eyes shut blindly!
The Son of Mary wept me,
The Son of Mary kept me.
In grey of morn,
Christ was forlorn!

O Countenance like the Ember,
Bid me remember
The Lamb of God, sore-taken,
The Lamb of God, forsaken,
The Lamb of God under clay
Three days till Resurrection-Day.
O Countenance like the Ember,
Bid me remember!

JAMES BURKE
(1877-1958)

Missionary Hymn

Go ye afar. Go teach all nations:
Bear witness unto me,
On earth in every clime;
And I with you shall be,
Until the end of time.
Lovely appear, over the mountains
The feet of them that preach,
And bring good news of peace.

Spirit Divine, Fount of all graces!
Thy chosen ones inspire,
With love their hearts inflame;
And grant them tongues of fire,
To witness Jesus' name.

Mary most pure, Queen of Apostles!
In pagan lands afar,
Mid darkness, pain and strife,
Be thou their guiding star,
Their hope, their joy, their life.

THOMAS McDONAGH
(1878-1916)

The Lifting of the Cloud

The church bells ring — it is the Sabbath day;
    And as I look upon the passing crowd
    Of faithful young and old, the wonted cloud
Is raised, and brighter memories to me stray: —
I mind the times I trod the trusting way
    That leads to peace, my spirit humbly bowed
    In faithful prayer, ere came the impulse proud
Which lured me on to trackless doubts' dismay.

I will arise and visit once again
    The home of hope and rest, and pray once more;
For there no contrite humble prayer is vain —
    Oh give me back my voice, my sight restore,
    That I may see and praise Thee as of yore,
That this, Thy light may in my soul remain.

Wishes for My Son
Born on St Cecilia's Day, 1912

Now, my son, is life for you,
And I wish you joy of it, —
Joy of power in all you do,
Deeper passion, better wit
Than I had who had enough,
Quicker life and length thereof,
More of every gift but love.

Love I have beyond all men,
Love that now you share with me —
What have I to wish you
But that you be good and free,
And that God to you may give
Grace in stronger days to live?

For I wish you more than I
Ever knew of glorious deed,
Though no rapture passed me by
Than an eager heart could heed,
Though I followed heights and sought
Things the sequel never brought.

Wild and perilous holy things
Flaming with a martyr's blood,
And the joy that laughs and sings
Where a foe must be withstood,
Joy of headlong happy chance
Leading on the battle dance.

But I found no enemy,
No man in a world of wrong,
That Christ's word of charity
Did not render clean and strong —
Who was I to judge my kind,
Blindest groper of the blind?

God to you may give the sight
And the clear undoubting strength
Wars to knit for single right,
Freedom's war to knit at length,
And to win, through wrath and strife,
To the sequel of my life.

But for you, so small and young,
Born on St Cecilia's Day,
I in more harmonious song
Now for nearer joys should pray —
Simpler joys: the natural growth
Of your childhood and your youth,
Courage, innocence and truth:

These for you, so small and young,
In your hand and heart and tongue.

OLIVER ST JOHN GOGARTY
(1878-1957)

The Airman's Breastplate

*(Part of the Lorica or Breastplate of St Patrick turned into rhyme
at the suggestion of an Army Air Force Pilot)*

I arise above the clouds
Armoured in the strength of God's
Presence and omnipotence
That can drive all evil hence.

I arise in Heaven's might,
In the splendour and the sight
Of the Sun; and with the ire
Of Lightning and irresistible Fire.

Stabilized upon my road,
Held up by the might of God,
With God's wisdom for my light;
Eye of God for my foresight;
Ear of God to help my hearing;
Word of God to give a bearing.

Christ before me, Christ behind me;
Christ to be my guard abounding
Against drowning, burning, wounding;
Christ in all I do and dare:
Christ in me to win His war.

The Fool

Since the wise men have not spoken, I speak that am only a fool;
A fool that has loved his folly,
Yea, more than the wise men their books or their counting houses,
    or their quiet homes,
Or their fame in men's mouths;
A fool that in all his days hath done never a prudent thing,
Never hath counted the cost, nor recked if another reaped
The fruit of his mighty sowing, content to scatter the seed;
A fool that is unrepentant, and that soon at the end of all
Shall laugh in his lonely heart as the ripe ears fall to the reaping-hooks
And the poor are filled that were empty,
Tho' he go hungry.

I have squandered the splendid years that the Lord God gave to my
    youth
In attempting impossible things, deeming them alone worth the toil.
Was it folly or grace? Not men shall judge me, but God.
I have squandered the splendid years:
Lord, if I had the years I would squander them over again,
Aye, fling them from me!
For this I have heard in my heart, that a man shall squander, not
    hoard,
Shall do the deed of to-day, nor take thought of to-morrow's teen,
Shall not bargain nor huxter with God; or was it a jest of Christ's
And is this my sin before men, to have taken Him at His word?

The lawyers have sat in council, the men with the keen, long faces,
And said, 'This man is a fool', and others have said, 'He
    blasphemeth';
And the wise have pitied the fool that hath striven to give a life
In the world of time and space among the bulks of actual things,
To a dream that was dreamed in the heart, and that only the heart
    could hold.

O wise men, riddle me this: what if the dream come true?
What if the dream come true? and if millions unborn shall dwell
In the house that I shaped in my heart, the noble house of my
    thought?
Lord, I have staked my soul, I have staked the lives of my kin
On the truth of Thy dreadful word. Do not remember my failures,
But remember this my faith.

And so I speak.
Yea, ere my hot youth pass, I speak to my people and say:
Ye shall be foolish as I; ye shall scatter, not save;
Ye shall venture your all, lest ye lose what is more than all;
Ye shall call for a miracle, taking Christ at His word.
And for this I shall answer, O people, answer here and hereafter.
O people that I have loved, shall we not answer together?

Prayer to Mother Mary
Written for his mother before his execution

Dear Mary, thou didst see thy first-born Son
Go forth to die amidst the scorn of men
For whom he died.
Receive my first-born son into thy arms
And keep him by thee till I come for him.
Dear Mary, I have shared Thy sorrow,
And soon shall share thy joy.

The Mother

I do not grudge them: Lord, I do not grudge
My two strong sons that I have seen go out
To break their strength and die, they and a few,
In bloody protest for a glorious thing;
They shall be spoken of among their people,
The generations shall remember them,
And call them blessed;

But I will speak their names to my own heart
In the long nights;
The little names that were familiar once
Round my dead hearth.
Lord, Thou are hard on mothers;
We suffer in their coming and their going;
And though I grudge them not, I weary, weary
Of the long sorrow — and yet I have my joy:
My sons were faithful, and they fought.

JOSEPH CAMPBELL
(1879-1944)

When Rooks fly homeward

When rooks fly homeward
    And shadows fall,
When roses fold
    On the hay-yard wall,
When blind moths flutter
    By door and tree,
Then comes the quiet
    Of Christ to me.

When stars look out
    On the Children's Path,
And grey mists gather
    On cairn and rath,
When night is one
    With the brooding sea,
Then comes the quiet
    Of Christ to me.

I am the Gilly of Christ

I am the gilly of Christ,
    The mate of Mary's Son;
I run the roads at seeding time,
    And when the harvest's done.

I sleep among the hills,
    The heather is my bed;
I dip the termon-well for drink,
    And pull the sloe for bread.

termon-well: sanctuary or holy place

No eye has ever seen me,
    But shepherds hear me pass,
Singing at fall or even
    Along the shadowed grass.

The beetle is my bellman,
    The meadow-fire my guide,
The bee and bat my ambling nags
    When I have need to ride.

All know me only the Stranger,
    Who sits on the Saxon's height;
He burned the bacach's little house
    On last St Brigid's Night.

He sups off silver dishes
    And drinks in a golden horn,
But he will wake a wiser man
    Upon the Judgment Morn!

I am the gilly of Christ,
    The mate of Mary's Son;
I run the roads at seeding time,
    And when the harvest's done.

The seed I sow is lucky,
    The corn I reap is red,
And whoso sings 'The Gilly's Rann'
    Will never cry for bread.

bacach: cripple
St. Brigid's Night: Eve of feast of St. Brigid: 31 January

O Glorious Childbearer

O glorious childbearer,
O secret womb,
O gilded bridechamber, from which hath come the sightly Bridegroom
     forth,
O amber Veil,
Thou sittest in heaven, the white love of the Gael.
Thy head is crowned with stars, thy radiant hair
Shines like a river thro' the twilight air;
Thou walkest by trodden ways and trackless seas,
Immaculate of man's infirmities.

Every Shuiler is Christ

Every shuiler is Christ,
Then be not hard or cold:
The bit that goes for Christ
Will come a hundred-fold.

The ear upon your corn
Will burst before its time;
Your roots will yield a crop
Without manure or lime.

And every sup you give
To crutch him on his way
Will fill your churn with milk,
And choke your barn with hay.

Then when the shuiler begs,
Be neither hard not cold:
The share that goes for Christ
Will come a hundred-fold.

Shuiler: vagrant, tramp

THOMAS KETTLE
(1880-1916)

To My Daughter Betty
the Gift of God

In wiser days, my darling rosebud, blown
To beauty proud as was your mother's prime,
In that desired, delayed, incredible time,
You'll ask why I abandoned you, my own,
And the dear heart that was your baby throne,
To dice with death. And oh! they'll give you rhyme
And reason: some will call the thing sublime,
And some decry it in a knowing tone.
So here, while the mad guns curse overhead,
And tired men sigh with mud for couch and floor,
Know that we fools, now with the foolish dead,
Died not for flag, nor King, nor Emperor —
But for a dream, born in a herdman's shed,
And for the secret Scripture of the poor.

PADRAIC COLUM
(1881-1972)

Fuchsia Hedges in Connacht

I think some saint of Eirinn wandering far
Found you and brought you here —
Demoiselles!
For so I greet you in this alien air!

And like those maidens who were only known
In their own land as daughters of the King,
Children of Charlemagne —
You have, by following that pilgrim saint,
Become high vot'resses —
You have made your palace-beauty dedicate,
And your pomp serviceable:
You stand behind our folds!

I think you came from some old Roman land —
Most alien, but most Catholic are you:
Your purple is the purple that enfolds
In Passion Week, the Shrine,
Your scarlet is the scarlet of the wounds:
You bring before our walls, before our doors
Lamps of the Sanctuary;
And in this stony place
The time the robin sings,
Through your bells rings the Angelus!

An Old Woman of the Roads

Oh, to have a little house!
    To own the hearth and stool and all!
The heaped-up sods upon the fire,
    The pile of turf against the wall!

To have a clock with weights and chains
    And pendulum swinging up and down,
A dresser filled with shining delph,
    Speckled and white and blue and brown!

I could be busy all the day
    Clearing and sweeping hearth and floor,
And fixing on their shelf again
    My white and blue and speckled store!

I could be quiet there at night
    Beside the fire and by myself,
Sure of a bed, and loth to leave
    The ticking clock and the shining delph!

Och! but I'm weary of mist and dark,
    And roads where there's never a house or bush,
And tired I am of bog and road
    And the crying wind and the lonesome hush!

And I am praying to God on high,
    And I am praying Him night and day,
For a little house, a house of my own —
    Out of the wind's and the rain's way.

A Cradle Song

O men from the fields!
    Come softly within.
Tread softly, softly,
    O men coming in!

Mavourneen is going
    From me and from you,
Where Mary will fold him
    With mantle of blue.

From reek of the smoke
    And cold of the floor,
And the peering of things
    Across the half-door.

O men from the fields!
    Softly, softly come thro'.
Mary puts round him
    Her mantle of blue.

Mavourneen: my little darling

BRIAN O'HIGGINS
(1882-1935)

The Mountain Altar

Around it the furze-clad hills arise
    Like guardians strong and brave,
As if from the world's unfeeling hand
    Its story to shield and save.
And they'll guard it there, with a kingly pride,
    Though the skies may smile or weep,
Those brave old hills with a tender care
    Their vigil of love will keep.

The ivy clings to the moss-grown stones
    With a loving, unchanging clasp,
As if to shelter the friend of its youth
    From the plunderer's ruthless grasp;
And it weaves a canopy overhead,
    Where the breeze in summer sighs,
And the tender raindrops filter through,
    Like tears from the weeping skies.

When our Faith was banned by a tyrant law,
    And our Altars in ruin lay;
When the blighting gloom of the Penal night
    Fell dark over Freedom's day,
On this ledge the Sacred Host was laid,
    And the hunted *soggarth* here,
Offered up to Heaven the Holy Mass,
    While the hounds of the law were near.

There has it stood through the changing years,
    Unstirred by the howling gale;
Unbending, stern, and dark, and proud,
    Like a knight in his kingly mail;
Around it the wintry winds have swept,
    And the croon of the summer breeze
Has often rustled its ivied robe:
    But 'tis little it cares for these.

It has conquered all that would crush it down
  In the reckless flight of years,
Since first the moss on the soft, green sod
  Was moistened with sorrowing tears
For the home destroyed and the Altar wrecked,
  And the true and the brave laid low
By the iron hand of a bigot hate,
  In the days of a nation's woe.

In those grey old ruins of our native land
  There are memories sad and proud;
They tell of the patriot's noble fight,
  And they speak of the martyr's shroud.
Oh, guard them more from careless hands
  Than you would from the winter blast;
They were left to the children of Patrick's race
  To tell of a glorious past.

WINIFRED M. LETTS
(1882-1972)

Boys

I do be thinking God must laugh
The time He makes a boy;
All element the creatures are,
And divilment and joy.
Careless and gay as a wad in a window,
Swift as a redshank, and wild as a hare;
Heartscalds and torments — but sorra a mother
Has got one to spare.

The Harbour

I think if I lay dying in some land
    Where Ireland is no more than just a name
My soul would travel back to find that strand
    From whence it came.

I'd see the harbour in the evening light,
    The old men staring at some distant ship,
The fishing-boats they fasten left and right
    Beside the slip.

The sea-wrack lying on the wind-swept shore,
    The grey thorn bushes growing in the sand;
Our Wexford coast from Arklow to Cahore —
    My native land.

The little houses climbing up the hill,
    Sea daisies growing in the sandy grass,
The tethered goats that wait large-eyed and still,
    To watch you pass.

The women at the well with dripping pails,
    Their men colloguing by the harbour wall,

The coils of rope, the nets, the old brown sails,
 I'd know them all.

And then the Angelus — I'd surely see
 The swaying bell against a golden sky,
So God, Who kept the love of home in me,
 Would let me die.

Irish Skies

In London here the streets are grey, an' grey the sky above;
I wish I were in Ireland to see the skies I love —
Pearl cloud, buff cloud, the colour of a dove.

All day I travel English streets, but in my dreams I tread
The far Glencullen road and see the soft sky overhead,
Grey clouds, white clouds, the wind has shepherded.

At night the London lamps shine bright, but what are they to me?
I've seen the moonlight in Glendhu, the stars above Glenchree —
The lamps of Heaven give light enough for me.

The city in the winter time puts on a shroud of smoke,
But the sky above the Three Rock was blue as Mary's cloak,
Ruffled like dove's wings when the wind awoke.

I dream I see the Wicklow hills by evening sunlight kissed,
An' every glen and valley there brimful of radiant mist —
The jewelled sky topaz and amethyst.

I wake to see the London streets, the sombre sky above,
God's blessing on the far-off roads, and on the skies I love —
Pearl feather, grey feather, wings of a dove.

JAMES STEPHENS
(1882-1950)

Donnybrook

I saw the moon, so broad and bright,
Sailing high on a frosty night!

And the air shone silvery between
The pearly queen, and the silver queen!

And here a white, and there a white
Cloud-mist swam in a mist of light!

And, all encrusted in the sky,
High, and higher, and yet more high,

Were golden star-points glimmering through
The hollow vault, the vault of blue!

And then I knew — that God was good,
And the world was fair! And, where I stood,

I bent the knee, and bent the head:
And said my prayers, and went to bed.

Christmas at Freelands

I

The Red-Bud, the Kentucky Tree
Bloomed the spring to live for me
In Freelands; and the Mocking Bird
— Nimble chorister of glee,
Sweet as poet ever heard
In a world of ecstasy —
Sang the summer, and the sun;
Sang the summer in to me.

2

The spring is gone! The summer gone!
The cardinal has gone away!
The fire-flies, dancing on the lawn,
— each a little moon at play —
Are gone, with summer, gone away!
And, where green acres were aglow,
Daisy munches in the snow!

3

A snowy field! A stable piled
With straw! A donkey's sleep pow!
A Mother beaming on a Child!
A manger, and a munching cow!
— These we all remember now —
And airy voices, heard afar!
And three Magicians, and a Star!

4

Two thousand times of snow declare
That on the Christmas of the Year
There is a singing in the air;
And all who listen for it hear
A fairy chime, a seraph strain,
Telling He is born again,
— That all we love is born again.

CATHAL O'BYRNE
(1883-1957)

'. . . There is a tradition in Catholic Ireland that on Christmas Eve each family puts a lighted candle in its window, so that if Saint Joseph and the Virgin Mary should pass they may know that within, beside a fire and a table blessed by the grace of God, a family awaits them. So it is that wherever I may be throughout this world, if a Bulgarian away from his homeland passes my house, he will find the candle of welcome burning in the window': from the Christmas Sermon preached by his Excellency Angelo Giuseppe Roncalli (later to become Pope John XXIII) in the Church of Saint Joseph, Sofia, on the eve of his departure for Istanbul.

Christmas Wayfarers

Redden the hearth and sweep the floor.
Let the candle through the pane be showing,
bring sweet well water, and leave the door
loose on the hasp, for who would be knowing
what poor soul lonely and travelled far,
walking the world on the naked highway,
might follow the gleam of the Candle Star,
and its welcome win in this lonesome byway.

So, for the sake of two who went out from the city
by bridle lanes down to Bethlehem
and who failed to find there, for love or pity,
a kindly soul who would welcome them,
redden the hearth, let the comfort-sharing
glow of the peat-fire shine fair and bright,
and may a tired poor Man and a Maiden wearing
a mantle of blue, be our guests to-night.

A Donegal Hush Song

God bring you safe from the death sleep of night,
  A leanbh mo chroidhe
  My heart's delight.
From the green-hill'd homes of the *sluagh sidhe*.

O'er the purple rim of a star-lit sea,
Through a leafy lane, o'er Moy Mell's plain,
Where dew-drops strung on a gossamer chain,
From blossomy boughs, swing to and fro,
And a round red moon hangs low, so low —
God bring you safe through the night to me,
      My heart's delight,
      A leanbh mo chroidhe.

God bring you safe from the death sleep of night,
      A leanbh mo chroidhe
      My heart's delight.
From the grey world's edge where the rose-dawn sleeps,
Through the white dream gates where the shy day peeps,
Down the silver track of the morning star,
To the yellow strand where the white cliffs are,
When each fairy foot in a fairy brogue
Is hastening away to *Tir-na-n-Og*,
God bring you safe to the dawn and me,
      My heart's delight.
      A leanbh mo chroidhe.

A leanbh mo chroidhe: child of my heart
sluagh sidhe: fairy folk
Tir-na-nOg: Land of the Young
brogue: shoe or boot

SIR SHANE LESLIE
(1885-1971)

Holy Cross

It is the bare and leafless Tree
Our sins once sowed on Calvary,
And mockers digged with trembling knee —
     Holy Cross.

It is the dead unpitying Wood,
That like a crimson pillar stood,
Where none unmoved unweeping could —
     Holy Cross.

O fearful sight foretold to man,
The cloven spar, the sacred span,
Where God's atoning Blood once ran —
     Holy Cross.

It is the Holy Gibbet Tree,
All stained with Love's last agony
And marked with awful mystery —
     Holy Cross.

What stains are these incarnadine,
What scars are these more red than wine
Of more than human Passion sign?
     Holy Cross.

It is the sunless stricken Tree,
Upon whose branches sore to see,
O mystery, died One of Three —
     Holy Cross.

What storm swept o'er its boughs that day,
When God to God did sorely pray,
And human guilt ebbed slow away —
     Holy Cross.

When earth shall smoke and sun shall flee,
Alone unmoved o'er sinking sea
Shall stand one all-redeeming Tree —
          Holy Cross.

Forest Song

All around I heard the whispering larches
Swinging to the low-lipped wind;
God, they piped, is lilting in our arches,
For He loveth leafen kind.

Ferns I heard, unfolding from their slumber,
Say confiding to the reed:
God well knoweth us, Who loves to number
Us and all our fairy seed.

Voices hummed as of a multitude
Crowding from their lowly sod;
'Twas the stricken daisies where I stood,
Crying to the daisies' God.

Saint Patrick

O Patrick, hail, who once the wand'ring race
Didst win to be God's faithful resting-place,
And Ireland's love to soothe his wounded face.
          Alleluia! Alleluia!

In dreams thou heard'st thy distant children cry
To bid thee, holy one of God, draw nigh,
Lest all the Gaelic clans but live to die.
          Alleluia! Alleluia!

Christ was thy sword, thy breastplate and thy shield,
And Christ the living strength, that helped thee wield
A sacred spell o'er hill and lake and field.
          Alleluia! Alleluia!

Christ was thine eye, and Christ thine ear and tongue,
And Christ the peerless song thy brave lips sung,
And Christ thy challenge to the Druids flung.
            Alleluia! Alleluia!

O lonely strife no man can ever tell,
The years thou barest cross and staff and bell,
To war with all the powers and hate of hell.
            Alleluia! Alleluia!

Yet Ulster's plain thou choosest for thine own,
Armagh thou madest be thy royal throne,
To holy Down thou left'st thy burying stone.
            Alleluia! Alleluia!

But now behold thy sons are scattered far,
Thy western children weary wandering are,
And lone thy priests beneath the southern star.
            Alleluia! Alleluia!

Yet comes a day to ease thy people's pain,
Thy saints shall rise from glen and sea and plain,
When thou with Christ, in glory com'st again.
            Alleluia! Alleluia!

JOSEPH MARY PLUNKETT
(1887-1916)

I see His Blood upon the Rose

I see His blood upon the rose,
 And in the stars the glory of His eyes
His body gleams amid eternal snows,
 His tears fall from the skies.

I see His face in every flower;
 The thunder and the singing of the birds
Are but His voice; and, carven by His power,
 Rocks are His written words.

All pathways by His feet are worn,
 His strong heart stirs the ever-beating sea;
His crown of thorns is twined with every thorn;
 His cross is every tree.

I saw the Sun at Midnight, rising red

I saw the sun at midnight, rising red,
Deep-hued yet glowing, heavy with the stain
Of blood-compassion, and I saw It gain
Swiftly in size and growing till it spread
Over the stars; the heavens bowed their head
As from Its heart slow dripped a crimson rain,
Then a great tremor shook It, as of pain —
The night fell, moaning, as It hung there dead.

O Sun, O Christ, O bleeding Heart of flame!
Thou giv'st Thine agony as our life's worth,
And mak'st it infinite, least we have derth
Of nights wherewith to call Thy Name;
Thou pawnest Heaven as a pledge for Earth,
And for our glory sufferest all shame.

The Stars sang in God's Garden

The stars sang in God's garden;
The stars are the birds of God;
The night-time is God's harvest,
Its fruits are the words of God.

God ploughed his fields at morning,
God sowed His seed at noon,
God reaped and gathered in His corn
With the rising of the moon.

The sun rose up at midnight,
The sun rose red as blood,
It showed the Reaper, the dead Christ,
Upon His cross of wood.

For many live that one may die,
And one must die that many live —
The stars are silent in the sky
Lest my poor songs be fugitive.

Saint Augustine

Question the beauty of the earth,
the beauty of the sea,
the beauty of the wide air around you,
the beauty of the sky;
question the order of the stars,
the sun whose brightness lights the day,
the moon whose splendour softens the gloom of night;
question the living creatures that move in the waters,
that roam upon the earth,
that fly through the air;
the spirit that lies hidden,
the matter that is manifest;
the visible things that are ruled,

the invisible that rule them,
question all these.
They will answer you:
'Behold and see, we are beautiful.'
Their beauty is their confession of God.
Who made these beautiful changing things,
if not One who is beautiful and changeth not?

PADRAIG DE BRUN
(1889-1960)

Translation by Máire Mhac an tSaoi

Calvary

I would make a vessel, ship, a boat,
I would go of that impulse to Calvary,
Were there nothing to find but the grass of the place
Where the Master's heart's blood was spent for me.

Loyal and tearful I would think there
Of the crowd and the day that put out the Sun,
Of Mary and John, of the sad Magdalen,
After scores of thousands had been and gone.

But let me take back with me this of His precepts:
There is none His disciple who cannot learn love.
If I do not pity the poor, or visit the prisons
I shall be left with no claim on the City of Grace.

Is it not You, Lord!

Is it not you, Lord!
Well I know you.

Since that afternoon at Emmaus always
There are two that walk the road
Their hearts on fire and eager
Hear Him expound the Bible
Until full recognition wakens
with the bread breaking.

But He also walks on His way
By his side who, single and lonely
Sadly confers in his heart
On problems insoluble —

How suddenly it can happen
That he is dissolved in compassion!
All that is hard in him softens
And he will know Whom to thank.

Lord, in the day when I shall feel alone
Be with me at the hour the light is fading.

GEORGE SEAVER
(1890-1976)

A translation from the *Didache*

Communion Hymn

Lord, as the grain which once on upland acres
Scattered abroad, was gathered into one
In this one loaf whereof we are partakers,
In the blest fellowship of thy dear Son:

So may thy Church dispersed through all creation,
Seed of the living Bread, thy holy Son,
Broken for us and for mankind's salvation,
From the world's ends be gathered into one.

FRANCIS LEDWIDGE
(1887-1917)

My Mother

God made my mother on an April day,
From sorrow and the mist along the sea,
Lost birds' and wanderers' song and ocean spray,
And the moon loved her wandering jealously.

Beside the ocean's din she combed her hair,
Singing the nocturne of the passing ships,
Before her earthly lover found her there
And kissed away the music from her lips.

She came unto the hills and saw the change
That brings the swallow and the geese in turns.
But there was not a grief she deemed strange,
For there is that in her which always mourns.

Kind heart she has for all on hill or wave
Whose hopes grew wings like ants to fly away.
I bless the God Who such a mother gave
This poor bird-hearted singer of a day.

God's Remembrance

There came a whisper from the night to me
Like music of the sea, a mighty breath
From out the valley's dewy mouth, and Death
Shook his lean bones, and every coloured tree
Wept in the fog of morning. From the town
Of nests among the branches one old crow
With gaps upon his wings flew far away.
And, thinking of the golden summer glow,
I heard a blackbird whistle half his lay
Among the spinning leaves that slanted down.

And I who am a thought of God's now long
Forgotten in His Mind, and desolate
With other dreams long over, as a gate
Singing upon the wind the anvil song,
Sang of the Spring when first He dreamt of me
In that old town all hills and signs that creak:
And He remembered me as something far
In old imaginations, something weak
With distance, like a little sparkling star
Drowned in the lavender of evening sea.

AUSTIN CLARKE
(1896-1974)

Martha Blake

Before the day is everywhere
And the timid warmth of sleep
Is delicate on limb, she dares
The silence of the street
Until the double bells are thrown back
For Mass and echoes bound
In the chapel yard, O then her soul
Makes bold in the arms of sound.

But in the shadow of the nave
Her well-taught knees are humble,
She does not see through any saint
That stands in the sun
With veins of lead, with painful crown:
She waits that dreaded coming,
When all the congregation bows
And none may look up.

The word is said, the Word sent down,
The miracle is done
Beneath those hands that have been rounded
Over the embodied cup,
And with a few, she leaves her place
Kept by an east-filled window
And kneels at the communion rail
Starching beneath her chin.

She trembles for the Son of Man,
While the priest is murmuring
What she can scarcely tell, her heart
Is making such a stir;
But when he picks a particle
And she puts out her tongue,
That joy is the glittering of candles
And benediction sung.

Her soul is lying in the Presence
Until her senses, one
By one, desiring to attend her,
Come as for feast and run
So fast to share the sacrament,
Her mouth must mother them;
'Sweet tooth grow wise, lip, gum be gentle,
I touch a purple hem.'

Afflicted by that love she turns
To multiply her praise,
Goes over all the foolish words
And finds they are the same;
But now she feels within her breast
Such calm that she is silent,
For soul can never be immodest
Where body may not listen.

On a holy day of obligation
I saw her first in prayer,
But mortal eye had been too late
For all that thought could dare.
The flame in heart is never grieved
That price and intellect
Were cast below, when God revealed
A heaven for this earth.

So to begin the common day
She needs a miracle,
Knowing the safety of angels
That see her home again,
Yet ignorant of all the rest,
The hidden grace that people
Hurrying to business
Look after in the street.

Pilgrimage

When the far south glittered
Behind the grey beaded plains,
And cloudier ships were bitted
Along the pale waves,
The showery breeze — that plies
A mile from Ara — stood
And took our boat on sand:
There by dim wells the women tied
A wish on thorn, while rainfall
Was quiet as the turning of books
In the holy schools at dawn.

Grey holdings of rain
Had grown less with the fields,
As we came to that blessed place
Where hail and honey meet.
O Clonmacnoise was crossed
With light: those cloistered scholars,
Whose knowledge of the gospel
Is cast as metal in pure voices,
Were all rejoicing daily,
And cunning hands with gold and jewels
Brought chalices to flame.

Loud above the grassland,
In Cashel of the towers,
We heard with the yellow candles
The chanting of the hours,
White clergy saying High Mass,
A fasting crowd at prayer,
A choir that sang before them:
And in stained glass the holy day
Was sainted as we passed
Beyond that chancel where the dragons
Are carved upon the arch.

Treasured with chasuble,
Sun-braided, rich cloak'd wine-cup,
We saw, there, iron handbells,

Great annals in the shrine
A high-king bore to battle:
Where, from the branch of Adam,
The noble forms of language —
Brighter than green or blue enamels
Burned in white bronze — embodied
The wings and fiery animals
Which veil the chair of God.

Beyond a rocky townland
And that last tower where ocean
Is dim as haze, a sound
Of wild confession rose:
Black congregations moved
Around the booths of prayer
To hear a saint reprove them;
And from his boat he raised a blessing
To souls that had come down
The holy mountain of the west
Or wailed still in the cloud.

Light in the tide of Shannon
May ride at anchor half
The day and, high in spar-top
Or leather sails of their craft,
Wine merchants will have sleep;
But on a barren isle,
Where Paradise is praised
At daycome, smaller than the sea-gulls,
We heard white Culdees pray
Until our hollow ship was kneeling
Over the longer waves.

MONK GIBBON
(Born 1896)

French Peasants

These going home at dusk
Along the lane,
After the day's warm work,
Do not complain.

Were you to say to them,
'What does it mean?
What is it all about,
This troubled dream?'

They would not understand,
They'd go their way
Or, if they spoke at all,
They'd surely say,

'Dawn is the time to rise,
Days are to earn
Bread and the mid-day rest,
Dusk to return;

'To be content, to pray.
To hear songs sung,
Or to make wayside love,
If one is young.

'All from the good God comes,
All then is good;
Sorrow is known to Him,
And understood.'

One who had questioned all,
And was not wise,
Might be ashamed to meet
Their quiet eyes.

All is so clear to them,
All is so plain,
These who go home at dusk,
Along the lane.

The Poetry of Gerard Manley Hopkins

Incomparable treasure, heart's blood spilt
Out of heart's anguish, high heart, all-hoping heart,
Child innocent, clean heart, of guile or guilt,
But heart storm-tried, fire-purged, heaven-chastened,
    (chart
Clear-mapped but course sore-battered), when the worst
Skies clashed, light flashed — God visioned, none the less
God terrible — from that too great cloud stress
Came rain, came words at last and falling fast.

And why? To blossom beauty, seeding truth
In stillness thirty years, the saturate earth
Bounty for bounty yielding; tempest ruth
Vindicate, (not despair that deals out dearth).
No havoc out of all's heart-havoc wrought
But only heaven comfort, pilgrim sought.

The Prayer of the Arab Physician

Beneficent but blind, my blood
Obeys its proper laws, though I
Have issued no directive, nor
Can give it thanks if it comply.

An edict from afar has laid
Its ukase on this willing slave,
Who, though it knows me not, must yet
Study my interest till the grave.

I am not it; it is not me.
Twain we remain without a doubt.
Yet it does all at my behest,
And has no motive me without.

Allah, Whose law the blood obeys,
Make me as faithful unto Thee
As, in its blind obedience, this
Slave of a slave has been to me.

C. S. LEWIS
(1898-1964)

Evensong

Now that night is creeping
O'er our travail'd senses,
To Thy care unsleeping
We commit our sleep.
Nature for a season
Conquers our defences,
But th'eternal Reason
Watch and ward will keep.

All the soul we render
Back to Thee completely,
Trusting Thou wilt tend her
Through the deathlike hours,
And all night remake her
To Thy likeness sweetly,
Then with dawn awake her
And give back her powers.

Slumber's less uncertain
Brother soon will bind us
— Darker falls the curtain,
Stifling close 'tis drawn:
But amidst that prison
Still Thy voice can find us,
And, as Thou hast risen,
Raise us in Thy dawn.

Prayer

Master, they say that when I seem
To be in speech with you,
Since you make no replies, it's all a dream
— Or one talker aping two.

They are half right, but not as they
    Imagine; rather, I
Seek in myself the things I meant to say,
    And, lo! the wells are dry.

Then, seeing me empty, you forsake
    The Listener's role, and through
My dead lips breathe and into utterance wake
    The thoughts I never knew.

And thus you neither need reply
    Nor can; thus, while we seem
Two talking, thou are One forever, and I
    No dreamer, but thy dream.

Love's as Warm as Tears

Love's as warm as tears,
    Love is tears:
Pressure within the brain,
Tension at the throat,
Deluge, weeks of rain,
Haystack afloat,
Featureless seas between
Hedges, where once was green.

Love's as fierce as fire,
    Love is fire:
All sorts — infernal heat
Clinkered with greed and pride,
Lyric desire, sharp-sweet,
Laughing, even when desired,
And that empyreal flame
Whence all loves came.

Love's as fresh as spring,
    Love is spring:
Bird-song hung in the air,
Cool smells in a wood,

Whispering 'Dare! Dare!'
To sap, to blood,
Telling 'Ease, safety, rest,
Are good; not best.'

Love's as hard as nails,
    Love is nails:
Blunt, thick, hammered through
The medial nerves of One
Who, having made us, knew
The thing He had done,
Seeing (with all that is)
Our cross, and His.

PATRICK O'CONNOR
(Born 1899)

My Prayer

My prayer it is that I have friends
    In the streets where the poor of Dublin live,
For hearts have there the kindliness,
    The tender grace sad days can give;
And there is seen in faces wan,
    In weary eyes, a faith-lit glow,
As in a picture I have seen
    Of some calm saint of long ago.

In Dublin town, at the evening time,
    In many an old, high Georgian room,
They will say the hallowed Rosary,
    Or in the church's ruby gloom;
And as through thin, worn hands the beads
    Move slowly, slowly round again,
Great were my joy if I but knew
    That my poor name was thought of then.

A shield to me and a comfort sweet,
    Whatever the road that must be trod,
Would be their warm remembrances,
    For these, indeed, are the friends of God;
And men, at the end, will see among
    Those to whom Christ a crown will give,
Faces that I have often seen
    In the streets where the poor of Dublin live.

The Lights of Dublin

Now all the lights of Dublin
    Are many and many a kind:
There's candle-light and carriage-light,
    And torches in the wind;

Lights in the Coombe's high windows,
    Glimmering lights on the Green —
By me, far flown from Dublin,
    Through many a dusk they're seen.

Now all the lights of Dublin
    Are friendly lights and fair:
They are haloed round with wisdom
    When they dream in an olden square;
Mirthful on rain-wet pavements,
    They can turn the gloom to gilt
When tatters and rags go dancing
    To an old street-organ's lilt.

But the lights of the faith of Dublin
    Are lights that will haunt the eye:
The lamp lit dim where they kneel to Him
    Whose Heart to their heart is nigh;
And the glory of Benediction
    When the blazing altars shine;
And above the street the flicker
    Of a tenement-dweller's shrine.

Now all the lights of Dublin
    In beauty shall endure,
While they take their flame from the altars
    And the glowing breasts of the poor;
Fine and fair be their gleaming
    That all the world may mark
God's grace in the lights of Dublin
    Streaming across the dark.

Exiles

Down where New York's a-glare at night,
    And faces strange and voices hard,
I met a man with dancing eyes —
    'I come,' says he, 'from Oughterard.'

Under the bluffs of Iowa,
    Missouri's muddy waters flow;
And there I met on a summer's day
    A wee, old man from far Mayo.

He sang through San Diego's night —
    The sap of shamrocks in his throat —
A lilting piece of an Irish song;
    'Oh, I'm,' says he, 'from Ballymote.'

Good folk, who never watched the coast
    Of Kerry slip beyond your ken,
God save ye, this Saint Patrick's night,
    And us poor wandering Irishmen.

JOHN IRVINE
(1903-1964)

On leaving Ireland, Colm-Cille first landed upon the little isle of Oronsay, but on climbing a height, he found that he could still see his native land. Immediately he took to his boat and settled at last on Iona only when he had satisfied himself that the Green Isle could be seen no more. A cairn was raised when he first landed on Oransay and it is still known as The Cairn of Farewell.

Saint Colm-Cille and the Cairn of Farewell

I will not climb these heights again,
For there are thoughts I would not wake,
Nor gaze across the sunlit seas
For fear my heart should break.

The oaks are green in Derry now,
The waves break on the Irish shore,
My grief that I must say farewell —
Farewell for ever more . . .

So dear to me the singing birds,
The emerald fields of Innisfail,
What matter where my head shall lie
A blessing on the Gael.

The white gulls tumble in the spray
And fill the air with bitter cries,
And wild the tumult of my heart
The longing in my eyes.

But row me to Iona's Isle
Though I am weary of the sea,
Beyond the far enpurpled hills
That will not let me be.

Invocation to Saint Bride

Dear Saint Brigid of The Kine
Bless these little fields of mine,
The pastures and the shady trees,
Bless the butter and the cheese,
Bless the cows with coats of silk
And the brimming pails of milk,
Bless the hedgerows, and I pray
Bless the seed beneath the clay,
Bless the hay and bless the grass,
Bless the seasons as they pass,
And heaven's blessings will prevail,
Brigid — Mary of the Gael.

The Little Pets of Saint Mochua

When Saint Mochua knelt to pray
Each morning at the break of day
There always was about the house
A rooster, fly and little mouse,
Three willing slaves to serve him well
And share his solitary cell.
The rooster every morn would crow
And waken him for matins, though
When he slept too sound to hear
The mouse came forth and nipped his ear,
And though he never had a clock
The mouse would call him, or the cock,
And if he had to leave a book,
From out some dusty hidden nook,
A fly with patience and with grace
Would sit for hours and mark the place.

Saint Fiacre
Patron Saint of Gardeners

Kind Saint! who loved the garden flowers,
Be not unmindful of the hours
Spent in unremitting toil
To trim the hedges, break the soil,
And work with clippers, trowels or rakes
Until every muscle aches.

May the slips and bulbs and seeds
Grow more bountiful, rank weeds
Be eaten up when summer brings
Snails, and flies, and creepy things,
And let the borders and the shrubs
Be colourful, and free from grubs.

May the leafy branches spread
A pleasant shelter overhead,
From the sun's persistent rays
In the hot midsummer days,
And when flowers droop and pass,
May colour linger on the grass
When trees do weep their tears of gold,
For Nature's gifts are manifold.

JOHN D. SHERIDAN
(1903-1980)

Joe's No Saint

Joe's no saint,
And I ought to know,
For I work at the bench alongside Joe.
He loses his temper just like another
— Days he'd bite the nose off his mother,
And when I call for a pint of plain
Joe's not slow with 'The same again.'
He gives an odd bob to the poor and needy,
But you wouldn't call him gospel-greedy
— You know what I mean? —
So if there's enquiries after he's dead
I won't swear to no haloes round his head,
For I never seen none.
When all' said and done
I don't suppose they give haloes out
To fellows who like their bottle of stout.

All the same, though,
I'm glad that I work alongside Joe.
For in the morning time I lie on
Long after Guinness's whistle is gone
And scarcely have time for a cup of tea
— As for prayers,
Well between you and me
The prayers I say is no great load —
A *Hail Mary*, maybe, on Conyngham Road
— You know how it is? —
The horn blows on the stroke of eight
And them that's not in time is late;
You mightn't get a bus for ages,
But if you clock late they dock your wages.

Joe, though
He's never late at all,

Though he lives at the far end of Upper Whitehall:
And I happen to know
(For the wife's cousin lives in the very same row)
That he sets his alarm for half-past six,
Shaves, and goes through the whole bag of tricks
Just like a Sunday,
Gets seven Mass in Gaeltacht Park
And catches the half-seven bus in the dark.

In ways, too, he's not as well off as me,
For he can't go back home for a cup of tea —
Just slips a flask in his overcoat pocket
And swallows it down while he fills in his docket.
I do see him munching his bread and cheese
When I'm getting into my dungarees.

There isn't a thing about him then
To mark him off from the rest of men
— at least, there's nothing that I can see.
But there must be something that's hid from me —
For it's not every eight-o'clock-man can say
That he goes to the altar every day.

Maybe now you know
Why I'm glad I work alongside Joe.
For though I'm a Confraternity man
And struggle along the best I can
I haven't much time for chapel or praying,
And some of the prayers that Joe does be saying
Those dark mornings must come my way.
For if Joe there prays enough for three
Who has more right to a tilly than me?

When my time comes and they lay me out
I won't have much praying to boast about:
I don't do much harm, but I don't do much good,
And my beads have an easier time than they should.
So when Saint Peter rattles his keys
And says 'What's your record, if you please?'
I'll answer 'When I was down below
I worked at a bench alongside Joe.'

Joe is no saint with a haloed ring,
But I often think he's the next best thing.
And the bus that he catches at half-past seven
Is bound for O'Connell Bridge . . . and Heaven
— You know what I mean? —

To the New Ordained

But yesterday and he was one of us,
Sharing the tumult of our boyish ways.
And now he is a priest through all his days

His late-anointed hands
Are wet with sacrifice:
His whispered breath
Can summon Christ again to mystic death.
He is a priest for ever.

Let not this glory dim, O Lord,
This fervour fade:
Always remember him whom Thou hast made Thine own anointed.
Keep his heart
From all the dust of earth apart.

And in Thine teeming comfort ever be
Strength to his frailty.

The Priestin' of Father John

They'll be priestin' him the morra —
Troth it's a quare world too!
For I min' the rascal that he was,
And the things he used to do.
Many's the time I chased him
When the strawberries were ripe

Though I own I never caught him —
He was faster nor a snipe.
He hit me with a snowball once,
And that same very hand
Will be blessin' me the morra —
Troth it's hard to understand.

Lord Richard from Kircubbin,
Who's a sort of far-out frien',
Is struttin' round this fortnight back,
Just like a hatchin' hen.
McAllister from Cargey,
Who's no more to him nor me,
You'd think to hear the chat of him
He reared him on his knee.
Tom the Tailor's nearly bet
From hurryin' on new suits,
And there's powerful heavy buyin'
On caps and yella boots.
The Square is thick wi' buntin' —
Man dear there'll be a sight
When the late bus from Downpatrick
Gets in the morra night.

Oul' Canon Dan, God bless him,
Will be fussin' fit to bust,
And the women batin' other
To get the blessin' first.
But, Canon or no Canon,
And I'd say this till his face,
For all his bit o' purple
He'll take the second place.
Sure even if the Bishop came
Wi' yon big mitre on
He wouldn't get the welcome
That we'll give to Father John.

The pains are at me constant now,
I seldom cross the door —
But I'm crossin' it the morra
If I never cross it more.

You can quit your scoldin', Julia,
An' sayin' I'm not wise —
Sure the sight of him will ease me heart
And gladden me oul' eyes.
It won't be easy bendin',
An' the oul' knees will hurt,
But I'll get down there fornenst him
In all the mud and dirt.

And if I get a chance at all
I'll whisper in his ear
(Och I'll do it nice and quiet
So that no one else will hear):
'If anything should happen me
Before you go away,
It's no one but yourself I want
To shrive me for the clay.
The oul' Canon mightn't like it,
For he's still hale and strong,
And I'm sure if he anointed me
He wouldn't do it wrong.
But I'd feel more contented
If the hand that helped me go
Was the hand that threw the snowball
Twenty years ago.'

PATRICK KAVANAGH
(1905-1967)

Advent

We have tested and tasted too much, lover —
Through a chink too wide there comes in no wonder.
But here in the Advent-darkened room
Where the dry black bread and the sugarless tea
Of penance will charm back the luxury
Of a child's soul, we'll return to Doom
The knowledge we stole but could not use.
And the newness that was in every stale thing
When we looked at it as children: the spirit-shocking
Wonder in a black slanting Ulster hill
Or the prophetic astonishment in the tedious talking
Of an old fool will awake for us and bring
You and me to the yard gate to watch the whins
And the bog-holes, cart-tracks, old stables where Time begins.

O after Christmas we'll have no need to go searching
For the difference that sets an old phrase burning —
We'll hear it in the whispered argument of a churning
Or in the streets where the village boys are lurching.
And we'll hear it among decent men too
Who barrow dung in gardens under trees,
Wherever life pours ordinary plenty.
Won't we be rich, my love and I, and please
God we shall not ask for reason's payment,
The why of heart-breaking strangeness in dreeping hedges
Nor analyse God's breath in common statement.
We have thrown into the dust-bin the clay-minted wages
Of pleasure, knowledge and the conscious hour —
And Christ comes with a January flower.

Canal Bank Walk

Leafy-With-Love banks and the green waters of the canal
Pouring redemption for me, that I do
The will of God, wallow in the habitual, the banal,
Grow with nature again as before I grew.
The bright stick trapped, the breeze adding a third
Party to the couple kissing on an old seat,
And a bird gathering materials for the nest for the Word
Eloquently new and abandoned to its delirious beat.
O unworn world enrapture me, enrapture me in a web
Of fabulous grass and eternal voices by a beech,
Feed the gaping need of my senses, give me ad lib
To pray unselfconsciously with overflowing speech
For this soul needs to be honoured with a new dress woven
From green and blue things and arguments that cannot be proven.

The One

Green, blue, yellow and red —
God is down in the swamps and marshes
Sensational as April and almost incredible the flowering of our
    catharsis.
A humble scene in a backward place
Where no one important ever looked
The raving flowers looked up in the face
Of the One and the Endless, the Mind that has baulked
The profoundest of mortals. A primrose, a violet,
A violent wild iris — but mostly anonymous performers
Yet an important occasion as the Muse at her toilet
Prepared to inform the local farmers
That beautiful, beautiful, beautiful God
Was breathing His love by a cut-away bog.

Ploughman

I turn the lea-green down
Gaily now,
And paint the meadow brown
With my plough.

I dream with silvery gull
And brazen crow.
A thing that is beautiful
I may know.

Tranquillity walks with me
And no care.
O, the quiet ecstasy
Like a prayer.

I find a star-lovely art
In a dark sod.
Joy that is timeless! O heart
That knows God!

I may reap

I who have not sown,
I too
By God's grace may come to harvest
And proud,
As the bowed
Reapers
At the Assumption,
Murmur thanksgiving.

CECIL DAY LEWIS
(1905-1972)

The Christmas Rose

What is the flower that blooms each year
In flowerless days,
Making a little blaze
On the bleak earth, giving my heart some cheer?

    Harsh the sky and hard the ground
    When the Christmas rose is found.
    Look! its white star, low on earth,
    Rays a vision of rebirth.

Who is the child that's born each year —
His bedding, straw:
His grace, enough to thaw
My wintering life, and melt a world's despair?

    Harsh the sky and hard the earth
    When the Christmas child comes forth.
    Look, around a stable throne
    Beasts and wise men are at one.

What men are we that, year on year
We Herod-wise
In our cold wits devise
A death of innocents, a rule of fear?

    Hushed your earth, full-starred your sky
    For a new nativity:
    Be born in us, relieve our plight,
    Christmas child, you rose of light!

Offertorium
From *Requiem for the Living*

O God, in whom we half believe,
Or not believe,
Or pray to like importunate children
Tugging a sleeve:
Whether man's need created you,
Or his creation seed from you,
Our creeds have overshaded you
With terror, pain and grief.

O God, in whose mysterious name
We men have lit
Age after age the torturer's flame
And died in it:
If you have not forsaken us,
Rake out this burning rage from us,
Give us concern, awake in us
Children a holier spirit!

The kin-dividing sovereignty
Of pride and fear, the blasphemy
Which is our blear-eyed apathy —
These let us sacrifice;
Burn up the false gods that infect
Our soul with lies,
Melt down the bars that cage us off
In cells of ice.

If you exist, if heed our cares,
If these our offerings and prayers
Could save, if earth's entreating heirs
Are to be born to live —
Spirit, in whom we half believe
And would believe,
Free us from fear, revive us in
A fire of love.

LOUIS MacNEICE
(1907-1963)

Prayer before Birth

I am not yet born; O hear me.
Let not the blood-sucking bat or the rat or the stoat
  or the club-footed ghoul come near me.

I am not yet born, console me.
I fear that the human race may with tall walls wall me,
  with strong drugs dope me, with wise lies lure me,
  on black racks rack me, in blood-baths roll me.

I am not yet born; provide me
With water to dandle me, grass to grow for me, trees to talk
  to me, sky to sing to me, birds and white light
  in the back of my mind to guide me.

I am not yet born; forgive me
For the sins that in me the world shall commit, my words
  when they speak me, my thoughts when they think me,
  my reason engendered by traitors beyond me,
  my life when they murder by means of my
  hands, my death when they live me.

I am not yet born; rehearse me
In the parts I must play and the cues I must take when
  old men lecture me, bureaucrats hector me, mountains
  frown at me, lovers laugh at me, the white
  waves call me to folly and the desert calls
  me to doom and the beggar refuses
  my gift and my children curse me.

I am not yet born; O hear me,
Let not the man who is beast or who thinks he is God
  come near me.

229

I am not yet born; O fill me
With strength against those who would freeze my
   humanity, would dragoon me into a lethal automaton,
     would make me a cog in a machine, a thing with
      one face, a thing, and against all those
       who would dissipate my entirety, would
        blow me like thistledown hither and
         thither or hither and thither
          like water held in the
           hands would spill me.

Let them not make me a stone and let them not spill me.
Otherwise kill me.

A Week to Christmas
From *Autumn Journal*

A week to Christmas, cards of snow and holly,
   Gimcracks in the shops,
Wishes and memories wrapped in tissue paper,
   Trinkets, gadgets, and lollipops
And as if through coloured glasses .
   We remember our childhood's thrill
Waking in the morning to the rustling of paper,
   The eiderdown heaped in a hill
Of wogs and dogs and bears and bricks and apples
   And the feeling that Christmas Day
Was a coral island in time where we land and eat our lotus
   But where we can never stay.
There was a star in the East, the magi in their turbans
   Brought their luxury toys
In homage to a child born to capsize their values
   And wreck their equipoise.
A smell of hay like peace in the dark stable —
   Not peace however but a sword
To cut the Gordian knot of logical self-interest,
   The fool-proof golden cord;
For Christ walked in where no philosopher treads
   But armed with more than folly

Making the smooth place rough and knocking the heads
    Of Church and State together.
In honour of whom we have taken over the pagan
    Saturnalia for our annual treat
Letting the belly have its say, ignoring
    The spirit while we eat.
And Conscience still goes crying through the desert
    With sackcloth round his loins:
A week to Christmas — hark the herald angels
    Beg for copper coins.

Rome Sunday June 1960

Expectant faces brimmed the waiting square
their Holy Father breasted his high sill;
incessant roars of greeting rocked the air
and swept with pigeons round each pinnacle.
The Holy Father spoke; the world stood still,
secure within the comfort of his care;
ev'n I, conditioned not to bend my will
to any dogma, felt that grace was there.

We'd stood an hour, midmost the rustling crowd,
on a plinth's vantage, critical, withdrawn
from fumbled cameras and rosaries,
yet, for that instant's mercy, we are proud,
and count among the moments of our peace,
we shared the blessing of that good Pope John.

Whit Monday

The small girls hurried to the hill-top church,
their confirmation-dresses fluttering
in the late sun. Before the shadowed porch
neat-fingered mothers knotted lace and string
and pinned each floral coronet in place;
while dark-suited fathers stood apart
pride and affection on each polished face;
it seemed as though some play were poised to start,
when the last swift had scoured the humming air.

Yet this was Poland and the time was now
and I, who pray too seldom, felt a prayer
take all my will, that providence allow,
or dialectic, or whatever name
men put upon time's enginery, permit
this scene to re-enact itself, the same,
so long as any heart finds grace in it.

Stable Straw

Straw, and figures of moulded clay,
the white-knitted hands of the men that pray
when Christian men make a holiday
for a Child, a Man, and a Lady.

The pith of out life, the ground of our awe,
the meat and the marrow of all our law,
symbolled in clay and in stable-straw;
a Child, a Man and a Lady.

For, all the beauty of tree and wind,
and the deepest thought of the stillest mind,
are driven dust, if the soul is blind
to a Child, a Man, and a Lady.

Clerk, deck altar, and kindle light,
and beat the bell in the tower's height:
priests are vesting in clothes of white
for God who was born a baby.

Immolation

On taut air — bells; lifted, adoring eyes;
and, sinner, seraph, *GOD*, look upon *GOD*.

Honour to Thee and praise!
Love unto Thee and praise!
Honour and love to Thee, O Lord, and praise.

Christ, star-told in the east,
Christ, lover of 'these least,'
Christ of the marriage-feast
in this White Host.

Christ by the Kings adored,
Christ come to bring the sword,
Christ the Incarnate Word
in this White Host.

Christ of the uncast stone,
Christ in the garden prone,
Christ agonized, alone .
in this White Host.

Christ with ensanguined cheek,
Christ from the scourging weak,
Christ with his mockers meek
in this White Host.

Christ of the supper room,
Christ of the empty tomb,
Christ of the Day of Doom
In this White Host.

Who was, before the Sun,
Who lived, ere Life begun,
Who shall, when Time be done,
in this White Host.

Who dreamed this realm of earth,
Who called the seas to birth,
Who made the stars for mirth,
in this White Host.

Who Glory is and Light
Who Majesty and Might
Who fullness of Delight
In this White Host.

Who dread Divinity
Who One in Trinity,
Who is Infinity,
in this White Host.

Jesu, with Magdalen I join my plea,
with him who craved remembrance
from the tree,
with drowning Peter: 'Lord deliver me'
by this White Host.

From *Sleep*

While now I lay me down to sleep
I pray to God my soul to keep:
never to let my body die
till Christ's Body in me lie,
till Christ's Blood behind the oil
leaving anointing hand assoil
lid, and limb, and lip, and ear,
and nostril, till the spirit's clear.
Ah then I'll lay me down to sleep
and Father, Son and Spirit keep
my soul until my body leap.
Until my body leap from clay
on all mankind's Uprising Day,
and down-sent soul and body sprung
shall rise together, rung by rung,
and I that was with worm and clod
in my own flesh shall see my God.

Lineage

Had *I* an inn at Bethlehem
I should have shut my door on them.

Had *I* hanged for theft on Calvary
I'd be deft with mockery.

Even if I'd been on Olivet
I'd have hidden it.

I *am* the boor of Bethlehem,
the hoist Calvary clown,
I was aloft on Olivet
and cringed in the town.

MAIRTIN O DIREAIN
(Born 1910)

Translation by the Author

Trees on a Frosty Night

Stripped of its leaves
Each tree tonight:
A sacrificial form
In presence of the Universe:
Its bareness is its dignity.

Each tree recalls
The Passion tree,
The tree of Crucifixion:

On each I see a figure stark,
Limb-stretched, heart-pierced —
The Christ rejected by humanity.

Invitation to Mary

Where will you find this year, Mary,
Shelter for your holy Child?
Every door is shut in his face
By the pride and hate of mankind.

Deign to accept from me
The warmth of my island home,
Away in the distant west
Where Atlantic breakers roar and foam.

There a heartfelt welcome awaits you
And a turf-fire burning bright,
And candles lit in each window
Bid the wanderer rest for the night.

CYRIL CUSACK
(Born 1910)

Cross Talk

'Himself on the Wood there,' says one,
'is surely the Son of His Mother,
a Man done undoing what's done.'
'He could be Himself', says another.

Said she, 'He's Himself is my own,
Himself only, born to be given,
bled whitest, white Bread of my bone,
red liveliest Wine for all living.'

Summer Reflection

Fly-flicking cattle-tail, quiet byre,
old rattle-rumbling tractor on the road,
a bold hallo, slow smile, a long blank stare,
wild antic light on hay, on boyhood hair . . .

child, careless of the frantic butterfly
at odds with air, aware less of God, fire,
of chaff and living grain, or of the load
of loss, of gain — again, that we must weep
for man by man enslaved, tied, chained
to a tired world that cannot sleep, nor die
to mean things meaningless that man has craved.
to hold which, sold himself, he cannot keep. . .

In this small piece of Eden, Saviour-saved,
still endlessly the stabled Babe will cry —
the lambkin calling on the straying sheep —
for a lost Paradise to be regained.

PATRICK J. MURRAY
(Born 1911)

God's Little Angel
(*For Fiona*)

From the moment of your birth
God took you to Himself,
Enclosed you in His arms
To guard you 'gainst whate'er
Might wound your angel innocence.

No word unkind shall ever pass your lips,
No thought impure shall ever stain your soul.
God's little angel, you
Shall keep that soul as white
As your baptismal robe,
As pure as driven snow,
Until He calls you home.

DONAGH MacDONAGH
(1912-1968)

Ballade which Villon made
at the Request of his Mother to pray to our Lady

Lady of Heaven, queen terrestrial
Empress you are of the infernal heath
Receive me now, your humble prodigal,
Who would be one of those about your seat;
Not easily elected the elite.
Your many gifts my mistress and my queen
Are even greater than my sins have been
Without such gifts no soul could qualify
To enter Heaven — here no lie I mean;
  And in this faith I wish to live and die.

Oh, to your Son make this memorial
That He may all my sins, as I entreat,
Pardon, as He made beatifical
Saint Mary, at whose prayer even the effete
Theophilus, who in his great conceit
Had sold his soul, was through that go-between
Pardoned and cleansed, who was the most obscene.
Grant no such sin be shared by such as I,
Nor to the sacraments to go unclean:
  And in this faith I wish to live and die.

I am a poor old woman, one who shall
Never learn now to read or write a sheet,
But in my parish church where paradisical
Paintings are on the wall I see complete
Heaven with harps and lutes, and hell beneath
Where damned souls are tortured; on that scene
I look with fear, the other is serene.
So, confident and joyful, I apply
To you for succour, my lady and my queen;
  And in this faith I wish to live and die.

*V*irgin, you bore our Saviour, Who has been
*I*n being forever and Who never shall,
*L*ong as infinity is, conclude His reign;
*L*ady, He left His Heaven and took all
*O*ur weakness on to help us to the sky.
*N*ow I pray to your Son, the Nazarene;
      And in this faith I wish to live and die.

SEAN O RIORDAIN
(1917-1977)

Translation by Valentine Iremonger

My Mother's Burying

A June sun in an orchard,
    A rustle in the silk of afternoon,
The droning of an ill-natured bee
    Loudly ripping the film of evening.

Reading an old dog-eared letter,
    With every tearful word I drank in
A raging pain stabbed my side.
    Every word forced out its own tear.

I remembered the hand that did the writing
    A hand as familiar as a face,
A hand that dispersed kindness like an old Bible,
    A hand that was like the balsam and you ill.

And June toppled backwards into Winter.
    The orchard became a white graveyard by a river.
In the midst of the dumb whiteness all around me,
    The dark hole screamed loudly in the snow.

The white of a young girl the day of her First Communion,
    The white of the holy water Sunday on the altar,
The white of milk slowly issuing from the breasts:
    When they buried my mother — the white of the sward.

My mind was screwing itself endeavouring
    To comprehend the interment to the full
When through the white tranquillity gently flew
    A robin, unconfused and unafraid.

It waited over the grave as though it knew
    That the reason why it came was unknown to all
Save the person who was waiting in the coffin
    And I was jealous of the unusual affinity.

The air of Heaven descended on that graveside,
A marvellous holy joy possessed the bird.
I was outside the mystery, a layman,
The grave before me in the distance.

My debauched soul was bathed in the waters of sorrow,
A snow of purity fell on my heart.
Now I will bury in my heart so made clean
The memory of the woman who carried me three seasons in
her womb.

The gravediggers came with the rough noises of shovels
And vigorously swept the clay into the grave.
I looked the other way, a man was brushing his knees.
I looked at the priest, in his face was worldliness.

A June sun in an orchard,
A rustle in the silk of afternoon.
The droning of an ill-natured bee
Loudly ripping the film of evening.

Lame little verses being written by me.
I would like to catch a robin's tail.
I would like to rout the spirit of those knee-brushers.
I would like to journey sorrowfully to the day's end.

Freedom

Translated by Coslett Quin

I'll descend mid other men,
Becoming pedestrian again,
Starting tonight.
Give me slavery I beseech,
Free from freedom's frantic screech
and my plight.
Let a chain and kennel bound
The packed thoughts that snarl around
My solitude.
Organized religion rather,

Temples where the people gather
At set hours.

So I've fallen in love with limits,
With all things with temperance in them,
With the derived.
With rule and discipline and crowded churches,
With common nouns and well worn words and
With stated hours.
With all abbots, bells and servants,
With the simile unassertive,
With all shyness,
With mice and the measured, the flea and the diminutive,
With chapter and verse, and things as simple as
The A B C,
With the drudgery of exchanging greetings,
And the penance of card-playing evenings,
And exits and entries.
With the farmer guessing at what wind
Will blow in harvest with his mind
On his field of barley.
With the common sense and old tradition,
And tact with tiresome fellow-Christians,
With the second-hand.
And I declare war now and ever
On freedom's fruits and all unfettered
Independence.

MAURICE CRAIG
(Born 1919)

Ballad to a Traditional Refrain

Red brick in the suburbs, white horse on the wall,
Eyetalian marbles in the City Hall:
O stranger from England, why stand so aghast?
May the Lord in His mercy be kind to Belfast.

This jewel that houses our hopes and our fears
Was knocked up from the swamp in the last hundred years;
But the last shall be first and the first shall be last:
May the Lord in His mercy be kind to Belfast.

We swore by King William there'd never be seen
An All-Irish Parliament at College Green,
So at Stormont we're nailing the flag to the mast:
May the Lord in His mercy be kind to Belfast.

O the bricks they will bleed and the rain it will weep,
And the damp Lagan fog lull the city to sleep;
It's to hell with the future and live on the past:
May the Lord in His mercy be kind to Belfast.

ROY McFADDEN
(Born 1921)

March

Stoned cheek turned again
The stone turned from the tomb:
Unvault spring
Like a lad,
For your parish needs hoeing
And a weeding of snakes
In constricted ground.

Aghast with ghosts in houses
Mothers and children stay
Tears for another day,
Since a corpse provided
Everyday.

Hold up your favour Patrick
Not like a riot-shield
Or clerics with their bibles
Or perpetrators' hands
Guilty of blood on the tarmac
Vengeance on old sick walls.

From Downpatrick Cathedral
(Abashed by daffodils)
Pronounce a curse on reptiles
Fused to ejaculate;

From Downpatrick Cathedral
(Three saints smudged on a wall)
Now that Easter flusters
From the shattered egg

Stained window-glass and rubble,
Chance another spring;
With hailstones maybe,
Or perhaps daffodils.

BRENDAN BEHAN
(1923-1964)

Translation by Ulick O'Connor

Repentance

In that awful hour when I'm on my deathbed
Stretched below on the cold bare board,
My friends and neighbours around me standing
And weak in my ears the whispered word;
In that time of affliction, O Mother Mary,
With no respite and my soul alone
But the saving grasp of your hand in my hand
On that trembling voyage to the Heavenly Throne.

That will be the time when my mind's tormented
With thoughts that crawl behind my eyes,
Following exhausted the glow of memory
Which lights the deeds of my life as they rise;
Calling my sins like an army sergeant
Mounting a guard against my prayer;
Don't ever abandon me, Mother Mary,
Without your grace as a shield to wear.

My sins will gather like greedy foxhounds,
Memory a horn to summon the pack,
And death on a horse, my life's course over,
The years safely ditched at his back.
When I'm run to earth and my lungs are panting,
At the hunt's end and death in my face;
Trembling, red-eyed while the hounds are baying;
O Mother, don't ever deny your grace.

COTHRAI GOGAN
(Born 1926)

Prayer of a Pagan Woman

God

You do not mind if I an unbaptized
Dare leave a coin amid the straw
Just at your feet.

You'll understand I could not join the Sunday show
of all the crowds.
I'll just sit here and watch my candle lighting
up your face.

How kind you look though just a tiny child . . .
All mine are big and strong
And seem sometimes unmindful
Of a time I carried them inside
Or on my arm, or riding up behind
To stream, to farm, to market in a line
By winding shady roads.

And all they've learnt . . .

Do you have room in your royal compound bright
For one old crone who cannot read or write?

The candle's dying.

But through the night-paths of the dead
be You my Light.

Mountain Drive
To Matilda, refugee, deaf and dumb

I see you now
with your great wide open eyes and quiet smile
absorbing the vast expanse of summer seas
and the purple solitude of rolling mountain-sides,
brown bogs with heather, yellow gorse and cotton white,
sliced by long black watery crevices.

Who taught you how to pray?
Your still wide eyes are open
round-wide, calm, reflecting, radiating
silent sounds to one who hears in silence.
How He seems to enfold you with His peace.

Does He speak to you in the soft sounds of colour, light and shade,
in the rough grey stone of this slight mountain chapel
where you sit serene?
The summer sun is dancing on the polished brown-oak seats
and glitters in the gloom of burnished brass and silver,
and marble veiled in violet, down to the rainbowed
windows.

Breezes swish the murmuring pines around.
Birds flute. Bees hum. A child cries far off.
The bleat of lamb.
But you, in your own great silent world,
you hear no word, except from Him.

CRISTOIR O'FLYNN
(Born 1927)

God?

Some men say there is a God
And others say no God exists
Because, they think, an all-wise Creator
Would not have made a world like this
Where children starve or die in pain,
Where want and hunger, war, disease,
Not to mention work and death,
Make the place a real valley of tears.

One thing we know: if there *is* a God
It's not *you*, certainly not *me;*
So, what this God would do, or why,
Is more than difficult for *us* to see.

There was one man who made this claim,
That he was God and God was he;
People believed him, though he never
Explained life's agony or mystery.
In fact, he lived like other men,
Was weary, wept like you or me,
And his plan for mankind included
Dying like a scarecrow on a tree.

But was *he* God? How do I know,
Or you? All *we* can see
Is how little he got
Out of claiming to be:
And that (we know) would not
Be true of *you*, or *me*.

Sainthood

Why are saints so difficult to recognize
In these days, not like in olden times
When we had a resident saint in each oak-grove,
A holy well in each townland, miracles galore?

By the law of averages, if, as philosophers maintain
And common sense agrees, human nature doesn't change
And we are the mixture as before, there must be
Saints somewhere, if only we had eyes to see.

But perhaps this new environment of nuclear tests,
Television and freewheeling whim is not conducive to
The cultivation of holiness? Even the shepherds seem
More vulnerable to fireflies of lust, to the common greed.

On Saint Michael's Skellig the light is an unmanned lamp
Guiding the vessels of commerce from bank to bank,
Aeroplanes descend on Aran, and in the hearth's sanctuary
Titillating farces have exorcised the rosary.

I thought I had recognised a saint in disguise
When a man I knew handed over, in God's name,
Money which was to have bought another holiday in Spain
For his wife and himself, to the paralysed.

That wheelchair beside the door of the travel agency
Became a burning bush: the collection box asked:
'If we must live without ever walking, how can
You fly to Valencia, and Ireland's roads at your feet?'

However, I'm in doubt again since that man's anguished
Wife, deciding he was unbalanced — she was in doubt
At first as to where that money went — walked out
On him, leaving him freedom and scope to practise
His madness or maybe (who knows?) his sanctity.

JOHN MONTAGUE
(Born 1929)

The Answer
For Christopher Ricks

How when one entered a cottage
to ask directions, the woman of the house
rose to greet you, not as a stranger
but a visitor:
    that was the old way
the way of courtesy.
                  Searching for Gallarus,
I crossed a half-door on the Dingle peninsula
and stood tasting the neat silence
of the swept flags, the scoured delph
on the tall dresser where even something
tiny like a two-legged, horned alarm-clock
was isolated into meaning;
                      while friendly,
unafraid, the woman turned her face
like a wrinkled windfall, to proffer
the ritual greetings:
                     Dia dhuit/
Dia agus Muire dhuit/
               Dia agus Muire
agus Padraig dhuit*
              invocation of powers
to cleanse the mind.
              Then the question
and the answer.
               'What did she say?'
I was asked when I came back to the car
but could only point the way
over the hill to where
                obscured in the sea
mist, the small, grey stones of the oratory
held into the Atlantic for a thousand years.

*Literally: God (Mary and Patrick) to you.

The Little Flower's Disciple
From *The Leaping Fire*
For I. M. Brigid Montague (1876-1966)

Old lady, I now celebrate
to whom I owe so much;
bending over me in darkness
a scaly tenderness of touch

skin of bony arm and elbow
sandpapered with work:
because things be to be done
and simplicity did not shirk

the helpless, hopeless task
of maintaining a family farm,
which meant, by legal fiction,
maintaining a family name.

The thongless man's boots,
the shapeless bag apron:
would your favourite saint
accept the harness of humiliation

you bore constantly until
the hiss of milk into the pail
became as lonely a prayer as
your vigil at the altar rail.

Roses showering from heaven
upon Her uncorrupted body
after death, celebrated
the Little Flower's sanctity

And through the latticed grill
of your patron's enclosed order
an old French nun once threw me
a tiny sack of lavender.

So from the pressed herbs
of your least memory, sweetness exudes:
that of the meek and the selfless,
who should be comforted.

THOMAS KINSELLA
(Born 1929)

Carol

Garden and gardener He made
And then for seed Himself He laid
    To rectify our loss.
O red the Spring on the cruel blade
And lily-white His body splayed
    In pity on the cross.

Haunting our harvest like a thief
He hides His flesh in every sheaf,
    His blood in every fruit,
But rank the weed — Our Saviour's Grief —
We nourish into thorn and leaf
    To live by the sour root.

His is the hunger of the pyre
The seasons wither on; admire
    His great and ghostly paces
About the fume of His desire —
How many souls retreat, retire
    And turn away their faces!

Meadows whiten, stores are piled.
Again in our icy barn the Child
    Sleeps before the play.
Adore Him, now our hearts are mild,
To profit us when we have whiled
    Our innocence away.

JOHN JORDAN
(Born 1930)

Lolek

Czestochowa, Jasna Gora, Auschwitz, Nova Huta:
Archdiocesan Cracow:
Symphony of ashed flesh and steel and Mary,
Uncountable dark nights in the factory of death,
Salvos of laud on the Black Virgin's White Mountain
The people of God keen from metal with metamorphosed hearts.

Expectancy and rose of Christ's fair state
You have known it all:
Grease-paint, desk, sledge-hammer,
Mickiewicz's mighty line,
More resounding than Wagnerian microphones,
Juliusz Slowacki who painted the clergy,
And Juan de la Cruz wrestling,
Parched in a tawny landscape,
With the Angel of Faith.

You expect much faith from Patrick's children
In this our pleasant land of Country and Western singers,
So great a hope as yours must find it.
And meantime — while the phones ring and the keys tap and the
      words spawn —
Let the chisellers and the unstained
Sing a carol for Karol:
'May Holy Ireland be holier,
Perhaps even made whole ?'

Lolek: Pope John Paul's boyhood name.
Chisellers: Dublin expression for street urchins.

255

CHRISTY BROWN
(1932-1981)

Good Friday

In and out among the narrow little ways of the town
    They dragged Him, bearded Man, and the
        gems of sweat
On His brow glittered like gold-dust
    In the merciless fire of noon-day.
Sticks flashed and thudded dully on straining flesh;
    Taunts, maledictions, words sharp
        with scorn and hate
Sank as fire into the tired brain;
    Spits bright with foulness ran as lava
        down His chest,
And the cruel, thin stones of the hillside
    Made the blood run from the stumbling Feet,
Staining the earth with a crimson glory.

    On they dragged Him, the cross's shadow on His back,
Up the waiting hill, as an animal to the slaughter-house.
    He gazed forlorn, with timeless pity
        upon the deriding multitude,
Sunk in the agony of betrayal, His denied majesty
    A crown of thorns girding the tranquil brow;
And there, Fatherless, they nailed Him to a
    beam of mountain wood,
And the pain-bright eyes gazed into the deeps
    of all that had been
        and was yet to be,
Surveying His world, His desecrated Garden, hanging
        from the cross
Upon a brooding hill, a bleeding Ecstasy.

MENOTTI VINCENT CAPRANI
(Born 1934)

The Prizefighter's Prayer

I ask You not for victory . . .
For somehow, that seems wrong,
But only for protection
And the courage to be strong.

Strength — not to conquer —
But just that I'll fight well
And prove myself a sportsman
At the final bell.

I ask you, Christ of Suffering,
That should I suffer pain
I'll offer it for all my sins
So that it won't be in vain.

And if, perhaps, he cuts me
And the bright red blood I see,
I ask that I'll remember
The blood You shed for me.

I need you in my corner
But likewise, in the other,
So that I'll remember
My opponent is my brother.

And I pray that You'll protect us
From injuries severe,
That we'll give the fans their value
And every cause to cheer.

And make each single act
Of either one be fair,
So no matter who the victor
In the glory both can share.

And if, by chance, he floors me
And the canvas I should meet
Like Simon of Cyrene
Please help me to my feet.

Then should a little glory
Somehow fall on me
Please help me to remember
That I owe it all to Thee.

Please help me go the distance
Through rounds with danger rife
Not only in the boxing square
But in the larger ring of Life.

So I ask You not for Victory . . .
For somehow, that seems wrong,
But only for protection
And the courage to be strong.

Strength of mind and body
So I'll fight each battle well
And the Referee will raise my hand
At the Judgment's Final Bell.

BRENDAN KENNELLY
(Born 1936)

The Pilgrim

I see a girl climbing the mountain
In a red blouse and blue jeans
Rolled up to the middle of her shinbones,
No shoes on her feet meeting the sharp stones,
Climbing among rocks, a smile on her face
Though her mind may be bleeding from old
And new wounds. In time, she accosts the saint
And in the silence a story is told,
A drop is added to the deepening sea
At the top of the mountain before she
Faces down to the world from that brief height.
Below her, for miles around, the fields
Are graves for sheep that never saw the Spring light
In grass kneeling to receive the bones and skulls.

TOMAS MAC SIOMOIN
(Born 1938)

Translation by the author

The Silence

When You build Your harp frame
From these — my bones,
And make of this skull
Its sounding box,
Make of these neurons
Its golden strings,
Make of my nails
A plectrum,

And, gripping me tightly,
Through a poet's mouth sing
Your song,
O Jesu mild, our Saviour,
What wonder then
Your eternal song
Beneath a fleeting syllable?

RAYMOND MURRAY
(Born 1938)

Translation by the author

Carmelite

*To Teresa. When I was saying goodbye to her I noticed ivy growing
inside the door of the convent.*

Taste now, dear Teresa, the living poison of the ivy,
a plant that has grown up out of the garden of God;
it is not bitter really but sweet,
a healing remedy, the bottle of blood;
although your sins may be visible still,
traced in the veins of the wind-blown leaves,
I think when the sun will cut its way
into the cloister of the shadowed souls,
when the wind puts its shoulder to the door,
that your anxiety will flee before your glance,
a winter shade darting away —
an ugly ghost reflected suddenly on a ruffled stream,
or the momentary closing of a bird's wings
behind stained glass.

You will get your fill to eat —
the red iron of love,
the cold silver of chastity,
the gold of sacrifice;
and remember that the streaks of pain
are deeply cut into that picture
of the soul pierced by the sword of God;
you will have plenty in very little —
cheap brown paint,
bare flags;
and music to listen to —
a little bell that is tugged,
a door that is quietly closed.

SEAMUS HEANEY
(Born 1939)

Saint Francis and the Birds

When Francis preached love to the birds
They listened, fluttered, throttled up
Into the blue like a flock of words

Released for fun from his holy lips.
Then wheeled back, whirred above his head,
Pirouetted on brothers' capes,

Danced on the wing, for sheer joy played
And sang, like images took flight.
Which was the best poem Francis made,

His argument true, his tone light.

Poor Women in a City Church

The small wax candles melt to light,
Flicker in marble, reflect bright
Asterisks on brass candlesticks:
At the Virgin's altar on the right
Blue flames are jerking on wicks.

Old dough-faced women with black shawls
Drawn down tight kneel in the stalls.
Cold yellow candle-tongues, blue flame
Mince and caper as whispered calls
Take wing up to the Holy Name.

Thus each day in the sacred place.
They kneel. Golden shrines, altar lace,
Marble columns and cool shadows
Still them. In the gloom you cannot trace
A wrinkle on their beeswax brows.

Contact

When I call to you, God,
it is only that I want to grasp
what you can offer; when you call to me,
God, I know you want
all that I have to offer, so,
I yield to the distractions.
Foreknowing this you planned
pain so we'd remember; for centuries
it hardly worked, until you
God, came to learn that pain yourself
so you'd remember. Now,
if I can only find the silence,
a sudden glance towards you
can be my truest prayer.

Offertory

We offer you, Lord, in our strong, our sensitive hands
to-day this bread:
this plough and plod, soft coaxing, collecting,
   the mixing and moulding, dull rumbling of trucks
      till the crates are all named for those countless lands;
from our proud, proud hands, o Christ, accept this bread.
We offer you, Lord, in our soil-cracked, our swollen hands
to-day this wine:
this fall, this crush, the strain, the pain
   o crumbling collapsing of flesh and the fierce
      dizzy dash of the blood of those countless lands;
from our weary, weary hearts, o Christ, accept this wine.

Then give into our hands
   your flesh
      to melt and merge with the soil and stones.

And give into our hearts
   your blood
      to seep through the sweat when the world groans;

that our earth may grow through its brightest blackest parts
a sight well pleasing to the Lord of lands.

ALCUIN (735-804). Eminent educator, scholar and theologian. Born near York, England. Became director of the cathedral school in 767. At the invitation of the Emperor Charlemagne he became master of the palace school in Aachen. He was later appointed Abbot of St Martin's at Tours. Poem (trs.): *A Sequence for Saint Michael* 34

FRANCES ALEXANDER (1818-1895). Born in Wicklow. Wife of William Alexander, Archbishop of Armagh. Published several volumes of religious verse. Her best known poems are the three selected for our anthology: *All Things Bright and Beautiful* 125; *There is a Green Hill far away* 125; *His are the Thousand Sparkling Rills* 126

WILLIAM ALLINGHAM (1824-1889). Born in Ballyshannon. His early years were spent in Northern Ireland as a customs officer. He was later transferred to England where he became the friend of the literary men of the day: Carlyle, Tennyson, Patmore etc. Published several volumes of poetry. He is best remembered as author of *The Fairies* and *Four Ducks on a Pond*. Poems: *The Girl's Lamentation* 129; *The Abbot of Inisfalen* 131

AMERGIN Cf. *Introduction* and note on page 15. Poem (trs.): *The Mystery* 15

ANGUS THE CULDEE (8th century). Culdee or *Ceile De* is the Gaelic for Servant of God. He was a monk of the monastery of Clonenagh, and later joined that of Tallaght, Co. Dublin. To him are attributed *A Calendar of Church Festivals* and *The Saltair na Rann*, 'the longest religious poem extant in Irish' (Eleanor Hull). Poem (trs.): *A Prayer for Forgiveness* 43

JOHN BANIM (1798-1842). Born in Kilkenny. Educated at Kilkenny College and at the Drawing Academy of the Royal Dublin Society. Distinguished himself at home and in London as a dramatist, poet and novelist. Influenced by Scott. His best novels are *Tales of the O'Hara Family* and *The Boyne Water*. Poem: *Soggarth Aroon* 97

EATON STANNARD BARRETT (1786-1820). Born in Cork. Educated in London and TCD. Entered Middle Temple but never practised. Wrote satires, poems, and a play. Publications include *Woman and Other Poems* and *My Wife, What Wife?* Poem: *Woman* 86

MICHAEL J. BARRY (1817-1889). Born in Cork. Called to the Bar. Active Young Irelander and regular contributor to *The Nation* until his imprisonment in 1848. After his release he became a police magistrate in Dublin. Writings include *The Songs of Ireland*, which he edited, and *A Waterloo Commemoration*. Poem: *Hymn of Freedom* 122

BRENDAN BEHAN (1923-1964). Born in Dublin. Educated at Sisters of Charity School and North Brunswick St CBS, Dublin. A housepainter by trade. Joined the IRA. Spent time in Borstal in England and in Mountjoy Gaol, Dublin. Studied Irish language in prison and lived for a time in the Irish-speaking areas of Galway and Kerry. Writings include *The Hostage, The Quare Fellow, Borstal Boy*. He died in the Meath Hospital, Dublin. Poem (trs.): *Repentance* 247

ROGER BOYLE (1621-1679). Born in Lismore. Educated at TCD. Fought for Charles I in the Civil War, but changed sides and joined Cromwell. After the Restoration he supported Charles II and helped to win Ireland for him and was rewarded with the earldom of Orrery. Writings include *Parthenissa, Treatise on the Art of War*, several plays and poetry. Poem: *On Christmas Day* 62

EMILY BRONTE (1818-1848). Daughter of Rev. Partick Bronte, Haworth, Yorkshire, the son of Hugh Prunty, farmer and shanachie (story-teller) of Emdale, Co. Down. Patrick changed his surname while a student at Cambridge. He, too, was a storyteller and profoundly influenced his daughters. Cf. *The Gaelic Source of the Bronte Genius* by Cathal O'Byrne. Emily's most famous novel is *Wuthering Heights*. Her poems are collected in *Complete Poems of Emily Bronte*. Poem: *No Coward Soul* 124

CHRISTY BROWN (1932-1981). Born in Dublin. Almost completely paralised from birth with cerebral palsy. *My Left Foot* was typed out with the little toe of his left foot! Published works include *Down All the Days, Come Softly to My Wake, Background Music*. Poem: *Good Friday* 256

PADRAIG DE BRUN (1889-1960). Born in Co. Tipperary. Ordained a priest in 1913. Educated at Rockwell College, Holy Cross College, Clonliffe and NUI. Further studies: Irish College, Rome, and D.Sc. from the Sorbonne. Professor of Mathematics, Maynooth College; President, University College, Galway. Published many translations from Latin, Greek, French and Italian into Irish. His last poem, *Miserere*, might be titled *Journal of a Soul*. Poems (trs.): *Calvary* 198; *Is it not You, Lord!* 198

JAMES BURKE (1877-1958). Born in Kilkenny. Educated at Blackrock College, Dublin, and Holy Ghost House of Studies, Chevilly, Paris. Taught Science in Blackrock College and later became College Bursar. A talented musician. Spent his last years as Senior French teacher in Rockwell College. Poem: *Missionary Hymn* 170

JEREMIAH J. CALLANAN (1795-1829). Born in Co. Cork. Illness cut short his studies for the priesthood in Maynooth College, and for the Bar in Trinity College. He retired to West Cork where he collected legends and folksongs. He died in Lisbon where he had taken a post as tutor. Sigerson paid him this tribute as a poet: 'It is Callanan's distinction, a great one — that he was the first to give adequate versions of Irish Gaelic Poems.' Poem (trs.): *Lines to the Blessed Sacrament* 89

JOSEPH CAMPBELL (1879-1944). Born in Belfast. Educated at St Malachy's College. Poet and Playwright. Lecturer in Irish Literature, Fordham University. Member of the Irish Academy. President of the Catholic Poetry Society of America. Publications include *The Mountainy Singer, Irishry*. Poems: *When Rooks fly homeward* 177; *I am the Gilly of Christ* 177; *O Glorious Childbearer* 179; *Every Shuiler is Christ* 179

MENOTTI VINCENT CAPRANI (1934-). Born in Dublin. Educated at Scoil Mhuire CBS. Engaged in the printing trade. Novelist and poet. Novels include *Polmarran Tower*. Has also written the story of The Little Company of Mary, *The Spirit and the Heritage*. Poem: *The Prizefighter's Prayer* 257

JAMES CARNEY (1914-). Born in Portlaoise. Educated at Synge St CBS, UCD and Bonn. Professor in Dublin Institute for Advanced Studies. Translator and editor of Irish poetry. Publications include *Early Irish Poetry, Medieval Irish Lyrics, Poems on the Butlers*. Poem (trs.): *The Question of Ethne Alba* 17

SIR ROGER CASEMENT (1864-1916). Born in Co. Antrim. Knighted for his exposure of abuses and exploitation of natives in the Congo and South America. Hanged for high treason in London because of his involvement in the Easter Rebellion. Received into the Catholic Church before his execution. *The Crime Against Europe* comprising his prose writings and poetry was published in 1958. Poems: *Lost Youth* 148; *Fragment* 148; *Forest Thoughts* 149

THOMAS DE CELANO (13th cent.). Born in Celano. Italy, Joined St Francis of Assisi and was his first biographer. The composition of the Requiem Mass sequence *Dies Irae* is attributed to him. Poem (trs.): *The Day of Judgment* 51

AUSTIN CLARKE (1896-1974). Born in Dublin. Educated at Belvedere College and UCD, where he became lecturer in English Literature. Poet, playwright, novelist. Founder-member of the Irish Academy of Letters. Writings include *Twice Round the Black Church, Collected Poems, Collected Plays*. Poems: *Martha Blake* 203; *Pilgrimage* 205

PADRAIC COLUM (1881-1972). Born in Co. Longford. Educated at local schools. Poet, dramatist, short-story writer. One of the early Abbey Theatre playwrights, he lived for many years in the United States where he was popular as writer and lecturer. Member of Irish Academy of Letters and the American Academy of Arts and Letters. Works include *Broken Soil, The Land, Thomas Muskerry,* plays; *The Poets Circuits, Wild Earth, Collected Poems*, poetry; *Our Friend James Joyce*, prose. Poems: *Fuchsia Hedges in Connacht* 181; *An Old Woman of the Roads* 181; *A Cradle Song* 182

SAINT COLUM CHILLE (4th century). Poem, ascribed (trs): *Prayer to the Virgin* 41

MAURICE CRAIG (1919-). Born in Belfast. Educated at Magdalen College, Oxford and TCD. Poet, architect, archaeologist. Poetry publications include *Black Swans, Twelve Poems, Dublin* 1660 to 1860. Poem: *Ballad to a Traditional Refrain* 245

CYRIL CUSACK (1910-). Born in Dublin. Educated at Newbridge College and UCD. Member of the Abbey Theatre Company. Plays leading roles in stage and film productions. Contributes articles and poems to literary journals. Published work include *Timepieces*. Poems: *Cross Talk* 238; *Summer Reflections* 238

CECIL DAY LEWIS (1905-1972). Born in Ballintubber, Ireland. Educated at Sherborne and Oxford. Professor of Poetry, Oxford. Member of Arts Council GB. Poet Laureate. Writings include *Collected Poems, Requiem for the Living. Buried Day*. Poems: *The Christmas Rose* 227; *Offertorium* 228

JOHN F. DEANE (1943-). Born in Achill. Educated at UCD. Graduated in English Literature. He taught for ten years but now devotes himself to writing and to *Poetry In Ireland*, the society he founded. Published work includes *Stalking after Time* and *High Sacrifice*. Poems: *Offertory* 263; *Contact* 263

SIR AUBREY DE VERE (1786-1820). Born at Curragh Chase, Co. Limerick. A friend of Wordsworth, who admired his sonnets. Wrote several long poems and verse tragedies, including *The Lamentations of Ireland*. He was a just and popular landlord. Died at Curragh Chase. Poem: *The Right Use of Prayer* 87

AUBREY DE VERE (1814-1902). Born at Curragh Chase. Son of Sir Aubrey. Educated privately and at TCD. Became a Catholic and was professor of Newman's Catholic University, Dublin. Author of many works in prose and verse. *Innisfail*, his most interesting poetical work, deals with important events in Irish history. Died at Curragh Chase. Poems: *Dominica Pentecostes* 113; *Feast of the Most Holy Trinity* 113

WENTWORTH DILLON, fourth Earl of Roscommon (1633-1685). Born in Dublin. Educated at the University of Caen. First literary critic to praise *Paradise Lost*. Died in London. Buried in Westminster Abbey. Poem (trs.): *The Day of Judgment* 51

LYNN DOYLE, pseudonym of Leslie Alexander Montgomery (1873-1961). Born in Downpatrick. Educated in Dundalk. Became a bank clerk and in due course was promoted to manager. A popular writer of plays, short stories and verse. Publications include *Ballygullion, Lobster Salad, Me and Mr Murphy*. Poem: *An Ulsterman* 167

WILLIAM DRENNAN (1754-1820). Born in Belfast. Awarded MA in Glasgow University and MD in Edinburgh. Joined the United Irishmen and wrote their Manifesto. Became a well known writer of patriotic lyrics. His collected poetry was published as *Fugitive Pieces*, 1815. Poem: *The Wake of William Orr* 82

ROBERT FARREN (ROIBEARD O FARACHAIN (1909-). Born in Dublin. Took MA in Scolastic Philosophy in UCD. One of Ireland's most distinguished writers. Poetical works include *Times Wall Asunder, The First Exile*. Poems: *Stable Straw* 233; *Immolation* 233; *Sleep* 235; *Lineage* 235

SIR SAMUEL FERGUSON (1810-1886). Born in Belfast. Educated at TCD; called to the Bar 1838; QC in 1859. President Royal Irish Academy. Knighted for public services. Writings include *Lays of the Western Gael; The Poems of Samuel Ferguson; The Forging of the Anchor*. Died at Howth, Co. Dublin. Poem (trs.): *The Burial of King Cormac* 108

FLANN FIONN (d. 705). The name adopted, it is said, by young Prince Alfrid of Northumbria while he was studying in the Irish schools. He was recalled to Northumbria in 685. Poem: *Alfrid's Itinerary through Ireland* 46

RICHARD FLECKNOE (1600-1678). Said to have been a priest. Author of several poems and prose works, including *A Relation of Ten Years Travel in Europe, Asia, Affrique, and America*. Was the subject of a lampoon by Marvell which suggested the title *Mac Flecknoe* to Dryden for his satire on Shadwell. Poem: *On the Death of Our Lord* 61

ROBIN FLOWER (1881-1946). Born in Yorkshire, England. Educated at Oxford and UCD. Lectured on Celtic Studies in Yale and the University of Chicago. Publications include *Catalogue of Irish MSS in the British Museum, Ireland and Medieval Europe, Gaelic Translations, Poems and Translations*. Poems (trs.): *The Good Man* 31; *The Scribe* 32; *The White Lake* 32; *The Lark* 33

ALICE FURLONG (1875-1946). Born in Tallaght, Co. Dublin. Lived a retired life, but was a friend of Yeats, AE and contemporary poets and writers. *Roses and Rue* contains most of her best poems. Poem (trs.): *Fragrant the Prayer* 169

MONK GIBBON (1896-). Born in Dublin. Educated at St Columba's College, Rathfarnham, and Keble College, Oxford. Served in RASC in World War I. Teacher. Poetic works include *The Tremulous String, This Insubstantial Pageant, The Velvet Bow;* prose works *Mount Ida, The Climate of Love*, etc. Awarded Doctorate in Literature, TCD. One of our most prodigious and prestigious writers. Poems: *French Peasants* 207; *Prayer of the Arab Physician* 208; *The Poetry of Gerard Manley Hopkins* 208

COTHRAI GOGAN (1926-). Born in Dublin. Son of Liam Gogan, noted Gaelic poet. Educated at St Mary's College, Rathmines, UCD and Fribourg. Member of Holy Ghost Congregation. Worked as a missionary priest in Nigeria; at present a missionary in Kenya. Works include *Come Deaf Now Hear*. Poems: *Prayer of a Pagan Woman* 248; *Mountain Drive* 249

OLIVER ST JOHN GOGARTY (1878-1957). Born in Dublin. Educated at Stonyhurst and TCD. Surgeon and throat specialist; Senator of Irish Free State 1922-1936; noted wit and writer. Publications include *The Ship; An*

Offering of Swans; Selected Poems; As I was going down Sackville Street; It isn't this time of year at all; I follow St Patrick. Poem: *The Airman's Breastplate* 173

OLIVER GOLDSMITH (1728-1774). Born in Pallas, Co. Longford. Educated in Lissoy, TCD and Edinburgh. Never completed his medical course. Did hackwork for editors and publishers in London but fortunately found time for the poems, essays, the novel and plays which established his place among the great writers of English. *The Traveller* and *The Deserted Village* are his two major poems; *The Vicar of Wakefield* his only novel; and *She Stoops to Conquer* his most successful play. Poem: *The Village Preacher* 77

EVA GORE-BOOTH (1870-1926). Born in Co. Sligo. Sister of Countess Markievicz and friend of Roger Casement. *The Little Waves of Breffny* is her most popular poem. Spent the greater part of her life in England. Works include: *Selected Poems, Broken Glory.* Poem: *A Heretic's Pilgrimage* 164

GERALD GRIFFIN (1803-1840). Born and educated in Limerick. Went to London and contributed to newspapers and periodicals. Encouraged and aided by Banim. *The Collegians*, his best known novel, was later dramatized as *The Colleen Bawn.* In 1837 he entered the society of the Irish Christian Brothers and taught for a short time in the North Monastery in Cork, where he died. Tennyson is said to have admired his poetry. Poems: *To A Seagull* 99; *To the Blessed Virgin Mary* 100

STEPHEN L. GWYNNE (1864-1950). Born in Co. Donegal. Educated in Dublin and Oxford. Leading member of the Irish Parliamentary Party. Novelist, historian, poet. Served in France during World War I. Awarded the Legion of Honour. *Collected Poems* published 1923. Poem: *On One Dying in a Convent* 152

SIR WILLIAM ROWAN HAMILTON (1805-1865). Born in Dublin. Educated at TCD. Outstanding mathematician and astronomer. Intimate friend of Wordsworth. Author of several works on science and mathematics. Knighted in 1835. President of the Royal Irish Academy and Astronomer Royal of Ireland. Died at Dunsink Observatory. Poem: *O Brooding Spirit* 104

SEAMUS HEANEY (1939-). Born in Derry. Educated at St Columb's College, Derry and Queen's University, Belfast, where he became lecturer in English Literature. Later he was Head of the English Department in Carysfort Teacher Training College, Dublin. Currently Professor of Poetry, Harvard University. Has won several awards for his poetry and is highly regarded in literary circles. His published work includes *Death of a Naturalist, Door into the Dark, Field Work.* Poems (trs.): *Song of the Soul that knows God by Faith* 54; and *Saint Francis and the Birds* 262; *Poor Women in a City Church* 262

JOHN HEWITT (1907-). Born in Belfast. Educated at Queen's University. Though 'an Irishman of Planter stock', John Hewitt is concerned with the problems that continue to bedevil social relations in Northern Ireland. His poetry reveals a mind that is open and unprejudiced, and that yearns for peace with justice. One of our major poets. Published work includes *No Rebel Ward, Collected Poems*. Poems: *Rome Sunday June 1960* 232; *Whit Monday* 232

ELEANOR HULL (1860-1935). Born in England of Co. Down parents. Educated Alexandra College, Dublin. Noted Gaelic scholar. Founder of Irish Texts Society. Author of *A Text Book of Irish Literature, Pagan Ireland, Early Christian Ireland, The Poem-Book of the Gael*. Poems (trs.): *The Song of Childbirth* 16; *A Prayer* 37; *I Lie Down with God* 38; *The Soul's Desire* 44

DOUGLAS HYDE (1860-1949). Born in Roscommon. Graduate of Trinity College, Dublin. Professor of Modern Irish, UCD. First President of Ireland. Gaelic scholar, poet, playwright, folklorist. Published works include *Love Songs of Connaught, Religious Songs of Connaught, History of Irish Literature*. Poems (trs.): *The Mystery* 15; *The Joyce's Repentance* 90; *Night Prayer* 91; *Blessed be the Holy Will of God* 92; *Christmas Hymn* 92; *The Graces of the Holy Ghost* 93; *The Merry Jovial Beggar* 94

VALENTINE IREMONGER (1918-). Born in Dublin. Educated at Synge Street and Colaiste Mhuire CBS. Trained in Abbey Theatre School of Acting. Member of Abbey Theatre Company and Gate Theatre Company. Won AE Memorial award for poetry 1945. Entered the foreign service, 1946. Accredited Ambassador to Sweden, Norway and Finland, 1964. Publications include *On the Barricades* and *Reservations*, poetry; *The Hard Road to Klondyke* and *An Irish Navvy*, novels; *Wrap up my Green Jacket*, a play. Poem (trs.): *My Mother's Burying* 242

JOHN IRVINE (1903-1964). Born in Belfast. University technician, writer, poet. Contributor to the *Capuchin Annual*, and many other publications. Published works include *Wind from the South, The Fountain of Hellas, A Treasury of Irish Saints*. Many of his delighful poems have been set to music. Poems: *Saint Colm-Cille and the Cairn of Farewell* 216; *Invocation to St Bride* 217; *The Little Pets of Saint Mochua* 217; *Saint Fiacre* 218

SAINT ITA (480-570). Called the Bridget of Munster. Poem, ascribed (trs.): *Jesukin* 35

SAINT JOHN OF THE CROSS (1542-1591). Born near Avila, Spain. Co-founder with St Teresa of Avila of the Reformed Carmelite Order, which he joined. He suffered imprisonment and torture at the hands of opponents of the Reform; his first poem, *The Dark Night of the Soul* written at this time. *The Spiritual Canticle, The Living Flame of Love*, and *The Ascent of Mount Carmel*, a commentary on the *Dark Night*, comprise his poetry and mystical theology. Canonised in 1726. Declared doctor of the Church 1926. Poem (trs.): *Song of the Soul that knows God by Faith* 54

LIONEL JOHNSON (1867-1902). Born in Kent. Educated at Winchester and New College, Oxford. Regarded as an 'Irish' poet because of his sympathetic interest in Ireland. One of his collections of poems is titled *Ireland*. Received into the Catholic Church, 1891. Died in England. Poems: *Saint Columba* 160; *Te Martyrum Candidatus* 161

JOHN JORDAN (1930-). Born in Dublin. Educated at Synge Street CBS, UCD and Oxford. MA, UCD; BLitt, Oxford. Short story writer, poet, broadcaster and literary critic. Publications include *Patrician Stations, Blood Stations, A Raft from Flotsam '78*. Highly regarded as poet and writer. Poem: *Lolek* 255

PATRICK KAVANAGH (1905-1967). Born in Co. Monaghan. Educated at local school. Left his little farm for Dublin 1938. Poet, novelist and journalist. One of the most important poets of the century. Works include *Tarry Flynn* and *The Green Fool* — autobiographical novels; *The Great Hunger* is his most important poem. Poems: *Advent* 224; *Canal Bank Walk* 225; *The One* 225; *Ploughman* 226; *I may reap* 226

GEOFFREY KEATING (*c*.1570-*c*.1646). Born in Burgess, Co. Tipperary. Educated at a local bardic school. Received classical and theological education in Irish College, Bordeaux. Appointed curate in Tubrid, Co. Tipperary. Famed as preacher and poet. Author of first *History of Ireland*, written while hiding from the priest-hunters. Writings include *Sharp-Pointed Shafts of Death* and *Key-Shield* or *Defense of the Mass*. Poem (trs.): *Keen Thyself Poor Wight* 57

JOAN KEEFE (1930-). Born in Ireland. Educated at UCD and University of California, Berkeley, where she taught Irish Literature in the Arts and Hermeneutics programme. Co-editor of *Poetry by Women* and *The Other Voice*. Poem (trs.): *An Answer to Thomas Barry* 73

JOHN KEEGAN (1809-1849). Born in Laois. Self-educated. Contributed poems to *The Nation* and other periodicals. Regarded as the most popular of the 'peasant' poets. *Legends and Poems* contains most of his work. Cf. reference in *Introduction*. Poem: *The Irish Reaper's Harvest Hymn* 106

BRENDAN KENNELLY (1936-). Born in Ballylongford, Co. Kerry. Educated at Trinity College, Dublin, and Leeds University. Professor of Modern English, Trinity College. Poet, novelist, broadcaster. Winner of AE award for poetry. Regarded as one of Ireland's major contemporary poets. Publications include *A Drinking Cup, Selected Poems, Collection One*. Editor of *The Penguin Book of Irish Verse*. Poems (trs.): *Christ's Bounty* 29; *Saint, Bird, Angel* 29; *God's Praises* 28; *Jesus on the Sabbath* 30; *On the Flightiness of Thought* 39; *The Pilgrim* 259

THOMAS KETTLE (1880-1916). Born in Dublin. Graduated at UCD and became its first Professor of Economics. Called to the Bar. MP for East Tyrone. Joined the Dublin Fusiliers in 1914 and was killed in the battle of the Somme. Published works include *The Open Secret of Ireland; The Ways of War; The Day's Burden; Collected Poems and Parodies*. Poem: *To My Daughter Betty* 180

THOMAS KINSELLA (1929-). Born in Dublin. Educated at O'Connell Schools and UCD. Presently Professor of English, Temple University, Philadelphia. One of Ireland's most important poets. Works include *Another September* and *Poems and Translations*. Poems (trs.): *Exodus to Connacht* 63 and *A Poem to the Sacred Heart* 75; *Carol* 254

RICHARD DE LEDREDE (14th century). Bishop of Ossory. Franciscan friar. Associated with *The Red Book of Ossory*, comprising the diocesan annals and some religious poems, including *The Festival* in Latin. Poem (trs.): *The Festival of the Nativity* 53

FRANCIS LEDWIDGE (1891-1917). Born in Slane, Co. Meath. Educated locally. Left school when twelve years old. Worked as farm labourer and ganger on the roads. Contributed poems to local newspapers. Befriended by Lord Dunsany, who recognised his talent. Killed in Flanders during World War I. Poems: *My Mother* 201; *God's Remembrance* 201

JOSEPH SHERIDAN LE FANU (1814-1873). Born in Dublin. Educated at TCD. The son of a clergyman and nephew of Richard Brinsley Sheridan, he became part owner of *The Dublin Evening Mail* and owner of *The Dublin University Magazine*. He was called to Irish Bar in 1839. Author of sixteen novels, most of them of the eerie preternatural type, including *The House by the Churchyard; In a Glass Darkly; The Watcher, and Other Weird Stories; Uncle Silas*. *Poems*, edited by A. P. Graves, was published posthumously. Poem: *Hymn* 112

SIR SHANE LESLIE (1885-1971). Born in Monaghan. Educated at Eton and Cambridge. Biographer, poet, dramatist, short-story writer, historian. Became a Catholic in 1908. Writings include *Songs of Oriel, Poems of Shane Leslie, The Oxford Movement, Story of St Patrick's Purgatory*. Poems: *Holy Cross* 192; *Forest Song* 193; *Saint Patrick* 193

WINIFRED M. LETTS (1882-1972). Born in Dublin. Educated at Bromley, Kent, and Alexandra College, Dublin. Poet, novelist and playwright. Works include *Songs of Leinster* and *Christina's Son*, a novel. Poems: *Boys* 186; *The Harbour* 186; *Irish Skies* 187

C. S. LEWIS (1898-1964). Born in Belfast. Educated at Malvern, Oxford. Fellow and Tutor of Magdalen College, Oxford; Professor of Mediaeval and Renaissance Literature, Cambridge. Most popular among his many publications are *The Screwtape Letters; The Problem of Pain; Mere Christianity*. In *Surprised by Joy* he tells of his conversion from atheism. He has also written some delightful stories for children. He died in Oxford. Poems: *Evensong* 210; *Prayer* 210; *Love's as Warm as Tears* 211

HENRY FRANCIS LYTE (1793-1847). Born in Ednam near Kelso, Scotland. Educated at Portora School, Fermanagh, and TCD. Took holy orders and was appointed curate of Taghmon, Wexford. Served in Cornwall, travelled in Europe. Died in Nice. Remembered chiefly as a hymn-writer. Poem: *Abide with Me* 88

GEOFFREY Mac BRIAIN Mac AN BHAIRD (*c.*1600). One of a bardic family of Ulster, all of whom were attached to the O'Donnells of Donegal. Poem (trs.): *Morning Prayer* 60

WILLIAM B. McBURNEY (*fl.* 1840s). Born in Co. Down. Contributor to *The*

Nation. Also wrote under the name of Carrol Malone. Died in the United States *c.*1890. Poem: *The Croppy Boy* 115

DENIS FLORENCE McCARTHY (1817-1882). Born in Dublin. Spent some time in Maynooth College. Called to the Bar 1846. Professor of English Literature and Poetry in the Catholic University. Five volumes of poetry and numerous translations from several European languages. Contributed to *The Nation.* Edited *Book of Irish Ballads* and *The Poets and Dramatists of Ireland.* His personal writings include *Ballads, Poems and Lyrics, The Bell-founder, Shelley's Early Life, Collected Poems.* Poems: *The Paschal Fire* 117; *The Voyage* 118; *The Pillar Towers of Ireland* 120

DONAGH MacDONAGH (1912-1968). Born in Dublin. Son of Thomas MacDonagh. Educated at UCD. Called to the Bar and became a District Justice. Poet and playwright. Publications include *Veterans,* poetry in several anthologies, including the *Oxford Book of Irish Verse,* which he edited with Lennox Robinson, and plays, *Happy as Larry* and *Step-in-the-hollow.* Poem: *Ballade which Villon made at the Request of His Mother to pray to Our Lady* 240

THOMAS MacDONAGH (1878-1916). Born in Cloughjordan, Co. Tipperary. Educated at Rockwell College. Taught in Pearse's school, St Enda's. Assistant Professor of English, UCD. One of the leaders in the 1916 Rising. Executed by military firing-squad. Author of several volumes of poetry: *Through the Ivory Gate; Lyrical Poems,* etc. Poems: *The Lifting of the Cloud* 171; *Wishes for My Son* 171

ROY McFADDEN (1921-). Born in Belfast. Lawyer by profession. Is represented in several anthologies including the *Oxford Book of Irish Verse.* Publications include *Swords and Ploughshares, Flowers for a Lady, The Heart's Townland.* Poem: *March* 246

PIARAS MacGEARAILT (1709-1791). Protestant poet. Lived in Ballymacoda neighbourhood. He tells us he forsook his faith for his children's sake. His lifelong remorse is expressed in his curious litany in honour of our Lady. Poem (trs.): *An Answer to Thomas Barry* 73

THOMAS DARCY McGEE (1825-1868). Born in Carlingford, Co. Louth. Became a successful journalist in America. Editor of *Boston Pilot.* Returned to Ireland and joined *The Nation* and the Young Irelanders. Forced to leave Ireland after 1848 rebellion. Settled in Canada and became a minister of state. Assassinated by Fenians in Ottawa. Literary works include *Irish Writers of the 17th Century; Life of Art MacMurrough;* and some poetry. Poems: *The Celts* 134; *The Celtic Cross* 135

LOUIS MacNEICE (1907-1963). Born in Belfast. Son of Protestant Bishop of Down and Connor. Educated at Marlborough and Oxford. Lectured in Greek in Bedford College, London University. Script-writer and producer for BBC. *Collected Poems; Autumn Journal,* etc. Poems: *Prayer before Birth* 229; *A Week to Christmas* 230

MAIRE MAC AN TSAOI (1922-). Graduate of NUI. A poet in her own right, most of her poetry is in Irish. Publications include *Margadh na Saoire*. Poems (trs.): *Calvary* 198; *Is it not You, Lord* 198

TOMAS MacSIOMOIN (1938-). Born in Dublin. Educated in Ireland, Holland and America. Lecturer in Biology. Publications include *Damhna*, etc. Poem (trs.): *The Silence* 260

JAMES CLARENCE MANGAN (1803-1849). Born in Dublin. One of the most tragic figures in Irish literary history. Educated in various schools. Worked in a scrivener's office, then as an attorney's clerk. He was happiest as librarian in TCD Library. Became a slave to opium and alcohol. Died of cholera in the Meath Hospital. Lionel Johnson wrote of him: 'If he be not Ireland's greatest poet, at least he has only equals . . . The poet of *Dark Rosaleen* is a great original poet'. Poems (trs.): *Alfrid's Itinerary through Ireland* 46; *Hymn for Pentecost* 101; *Gone in the Wind* 102

KUNO MEYER (1858-1919). Born in Hamburg. Educated at Leipzig University. Lecturer in Teutonic Languages, Liverpool University. Co-founder and director of the Summer School of Irish Learning. His translations include *Ancient Irish Poetry, The Voyage of Bran, Triads of Ireland*. Poems (trs.): *Saint Patrick's Breastplate* 19; *The Song of the Woman* 24; *The Worship of Cromm Cruaich* 25; *The Hermit's Song* 36; *Prayer to the Virgin* 41; *The Crucifixion* 45; *Hospitality in Ancient Ireland* 48

SUSAN LANGSTAFF MITCHELL (1866-1926). Born in Carrick-on-Shannon, Co. Leitrim. Educated at private school in Dublin. In 1901 she became assistant editor of the *Irish Homestead*. AE was the editor and his influence can be detected in her verse. Published works include *The Living Chalice & Other Poems; Religious Verse* 1908; *Frankincense & Myrrh*. Poems: *Immortality* 158; *The Descent of the Child* 159

JOHN MONTAGUE (1929-). Born in New York. Educated at UCD. Lived in Paris for some years. His social and cultural background is Northern Ireland. Like Hewitt, he is conscious of the social divisions and inequalities. He is at present attached to the English faculty at UCC. Published work includes *Poisoned Lands; A Slow Dance; The Great Cloak*. Poems: *The Answer* 252; *The Little Flower's Disciple* 253

THOMAS MOORE (1779-1852). Born in Dublin, Aungier Street. Educated at TCD. Friend of Robert Emmet. He studied law in London and held a government post in Bermuda. On his return to London he was accepted in high society. His fame rests on his Irish melodies, still popular. He supported in word and in writing the struggle for Catholic emancipation. He died in Wilts, England. Poems: *Thy Heaven* 84; *The Irish Peasant to his Mistress* 84; *The Bird let loose* 85

PATRICK MURRAY (1911-). Born in Drogheda. Educated at St Patrick's College, Armagh, Blackrock College, Holy Ghost Scholasticate, UCD. Ordained priest in 1941. Dean of Studies at St Mary's College and Rockwell College.

Taught English literature. Contributed articles to newspapers and periodicals. Publications: *Poems for Pleasure; Reading for Pleasure; Mary, A Marian Anthology*. Poem: *God's Little Angel* 239

RAYMOND MURRAY (1938-). Born in Co. Armagh. Educated at Abbey CBS, St Patrick's College and Maynooth College. Ordained priest for the Archdiocese of Armagh. Awarded several prizes for his poems. Authority on local history. Poem (trs.): *Carmelite* 261

EOIN NEESON (1927-). Poet, novelist, historian. Published works include *The Civil War in Ireland, Book of Irish Myths and Legends, The Life and Death of Michael Colllns*, etc. Poem (trs.): *A Prayer for Forgiveness* 43

CATHAL O'BYRNE (1883-1957). Born in Belfast. Writer, poet and popular entertainer and lecturer. Authority on local history, especially that of his native city. His published works include *As I Roved Out, The Gaelic Source of the Bronte Genius*, and several collections of poems. Poems: *Christmas Wayfarers* 190; *A Donegal Hush Song* 190

SEAN O COILEAN (1754-1816). Poet of the Penal Age. A schoolmaster of Mycross. His *Timoleague*, often compared with Gray's *Elegy in a Country Churchyard*, 'must rank as an Irish classic' — de Blacam, *Gaelic Literature Surveyed*. Poem (trs.): *Lament for Timoleague* 80

FRANK O'CONNOR, pseudonym of Michael O'Donovan (1903-1966). Born in Cork City. Educated at CBS Cork and UCC. Daniel Corkery was one of his teachers. Fought in War of Independence. Lecturer TCD. Best known for his short stories — *Guests of the Nation*, etc. — and verse translations from the Irish — *Kings, Lords & Commons* etc. Poems (trs.): *The Sweetness of Nature* 22; *In Praise of Fionn* 23

PATRICK O'CONNOR (1899-). Born in Dublin. Educated at Belvedere College, UCD and Dalgan Park. Ordained priest in Society of St Columba, 1919. Served as missionary in Far East. Chief Far East correspondent for NCWC News Service during the wars in Korea and Indo-China. His best known poems are in *Songs of Youth and Later Poems*. Poems: *My Prayer* 213; *The Lights of Dublin* 213; *Exiles* 214

ULICK O'CONNOR (1928-). Born in Dublin. Educated at St Mary's College, UCD and Loyola. Barrister, biographer, playwright, poet, broadcaster. Published works include *Sputnik and Other Poems, Oliver St John Gogarty*, a biography, *A Terrible Beauty*. Poems (trs.): *Repentance* 247

EUGENE O'CURRY (1796-1862). Born in Co. Clare. Worked in The Royal Irish Academy and TCD for Ordnance Survey of Ireland. Lectured under Newman's patronage in the Catholic University. 'He and John O'Donovan re-established in Ireland after nearly two centuries of oblivion the ancient scholarship' — de Blacam. Poem (trs.): *Litany to Our Lady* 27

DONNCHADH MOR O DALA (-1244). Lived at Finnyvarra, Co. Clare. Buried at Boyle Monastery, Co. Roscommon. Many of his poems are addressed to our Lady. 'Undoubtedly the greatest religious poet Ireland has produced' — Eleanor Hull. Poems (trs.): *At Saint Patrick's Purgatory* 49; *Fair is Our Lord's Own City* 50

MARTIN O DIREAIN (1910-). Born in the Aran Islands. Educated at Scoil Eoghanachta. Moved from Galway to Dublin in 1937 and entered the Department of Education. Registrar of National College of Art. Poet-in-Residence, UCG. Author of eight volumes of verse and a book of prose essays. Winner of international prizes for poetry. Hon. D.Litt NUI, 1978. Publications include *Ar Ré Dhearóil; Saothar Próis*, etc. Poems (trs.): *Trees on a Frosty Night* 237; *Invitation to Mary* 237

SEAN O'FAOLAIN (1900-). Born in Cork. Educated at Presentation College, UCC and Harvard. Fought on Republican side in the Civil War. Lecturer in English at Boston College and Strawberry Hill Teachers' Training College, London. Short story writer, novelist, poet, biographer and historian. Published works include *The Stories of Sean O'Faolain,King of the Beggars, De Valera, The Silver Branch*, etc. Poem (trs.): *At Saint Patrick's Purgatory* 49

CRISTOIR O'FLYNN (1927-). Born in Limerick. Educated at UCD and TCD. Worked in England and Ireland as teacher, broadcaster, journalist. Published work includes *Sanctuary Island* — short stories; *Land of the Living & The Order of Melchizedek* — plays; *Banana* — poems. Poem: *God?* 250; *Sainthood* 251

BRIAN O'HIGGINS (1882-1935). Born in Co. Meath. Worked as travelling teacher for the Gaelic League. Later established a successful publishing business in Dublin. Works include *Fun o' the Forge* — humorous stories, and several collections of popular verse, including *Glen na Smol*. Poem: *The Mountain Altar* 184

FEAR DORCHA O MEALLAIN (*c.* 1650). Cf. note on page 63. Poem (trs.): *Exodus to Connacht* 63

MOIRA O'NEILL, pseudonym of Agnes Nesta Shakespeare Higginson (1870-1955). Married Walter Clermont Skrine. Lived for some time in Canada. *Songs of the Glens of Antrim* is her best known work. Poem: *Grace for Light* 166

JOHN BOYLE O'REILLY (1844-1890). Born in Dowth, near Drogheda. Joined the British Army as IRB agent. Escaped from Australian convict settlement and took up literary work in Boston. Edited *Boston Pilot*. Author of *Moondyne*, a novel, and *Collected Poems*. Died Boston. Poems: *The Infinite* 138; *The Lure* 138

CONOR O'RIORDAIN (18th century). Born in Co. Cork. Taught classics and other subjects to the youth of Macroom. *Hymn to the Virgin Mary* is the Epilogue to a Confession or Meditation in a Country Churchyard written in the same year, 1750, as Gray's *Elegy*. Poem (trs.): *Hymn to the Virgin Mary* 79

SEAN O RIORDAIN (1917-1977). Born in Ballyvourney, Co. Cork. Educated at a local school and North Monastery CBS, Cork. Member of Cork Corporation staff until forced by ill-health to resign, 1965. He was a part-time member of UCG staff for some years before his death. Publications include *Eirable Spide-óige, Brosna, Linte Liombo*. With Rev. S. S. O'Conghaile he published *Rí na nUile*. He received an honorary doctorate from NUI for his contribution to Irish literature. Poems (trs.): *My Mother's Burying* 242; *Freedom* 243

ARTHUR O'SHAUGHNESSY (1844-1881). Born in Dublin. Employed in the Natural History Department of the British Museum. Inspired by French poets and influenced by the Pre-Raphaelite school of Holman Hunt, the Rossettis, etc. Poem: *The Line of Beauty* 137

TEIG GAELACH O'SULLIVAN (1715-1799). Born in Kerry or Limerick. Lived in Waterford. Friend of Edmund Ignatius Rice, founder of the Irish Christian Brothers. 'Supreme among the late writers as a religious poet' — de Blacam. *To the Sacred Heart* is his most beautiful poem. Poem (trs.): *A Poem to the Sacred Heart* 75

EDWARD ARTHUR HENRY PAKENHAM, sixth Earl of Longford (1902-1961). Educated at Eton and Oxford. Dramatist, producer, translator. Associated with The Gate Theatre which he supported financially for many years. Classical scholar and fluent Irish speaker. Writings include plays (*Carmilla, Yahoo*, etc.), translations (*The Midnight Court, Doves in the Castle*), etc. Poem (trs.): *Morning Prayer* 60

SAINT PATRICK (5th century). Poem, ascribed (trs.): *St Patrick's Breastplate*, also known as *The Deer's Cry* 19

PADRAIC PEARSE (1879-1916). Born in Dublin. Educated at CBS Westland Row and the Royal University. Poet, playwright, essayist. Founded St Enda's College, Rathfarnham, to promote Irish culture and the Irish language. Executed in 1916 for his leading role in the Easter Rising. His *Collected Works* was published in 1917. Poems (trs.): *The Keening of Mary* 95; *Keen Thyself, Poor Wight* 57; *The Fool* 174; *The Mother* 175

JOSEPH MARY PLUNKETT (1887-1916). Born in Dublin. Educated at Belvedere College and NUI. Editor *Irish Review*. His study of the mystics St John of the Cross, St Teresa of Avila and St Francis de Sales is discernible in his poetry. Close friend of MacDonagh and Pearse. Executed for his part in the 1916 Rising. Publications: *The Circle and the Sword* and *Complete Poems*. Poems: *I see His Blood upon the Rose* 195; *I saw the Sun at Midnight rising red* 195; *Saint Augustine* 196; *The Stars sang in God's Garden* 196

COSLETT WILLIAM CHARLES QUIN (1907-). Born in Co. Antrim. Educated at Mourne Grange, St Columba's Rathfarnham, Campbell College and UCD. Professor Biblical Greek TCD. Many published translations from Greek,

Latin, Gaelic, and modern European languages. Canon of St Patrick's Cathedral, Dublin. Poems (trs.): *Fair is Our Lord's Own City* 50; *Freedom* 243

GEORGE RUSSELL, 'AE' (1867-1935). Born in Lurgan, Co. Armagh. Educated at Rathmines School, Dublin. Organiser for Irish Agricultural Co-operative Movement. His pre-occupation with theosophy tends to obscure the meaning of his poetry. Published work includes *Collected Poems, House of the Titans, Gods of War, The Avatars*, etc. Poems: *Immortality* 162; *Prayer* 162; *Desire* 163

GEORGE SEAVER (1890-1976). Born in Cheltenham. Sometime Dean of Ossory. Educated at Rossall and Oxford. Canon of St Patrick's Cathedral, Dublin. Traveller and biographer. Works include *Edward Wilson of the Antarctic; Scott of the Antarctic*, etc. Died in Greystones, Co. Wicklow. Poem (trs.) adapted from the Didache, a document discovered in Istanbul in 1883 and believed to belong to the later years of the first century and to contain the teaching of the Twelve Apostles: *Communion Hymn* 200

JOHN D. SHERIDAN (1903-1980). Born in Glasgow. Educated at O'Connell Schools, Dublin, St Patrick's Teacher Training College, and UCD. He enjoyed wide popularity as a writer of humorous essays. Poems: *Joe's No Saint* 219; *The Priestin' of Father John* 221; *To the New Ordained* 221

DORA SIGERSON SHORTER (1866-1917). Daughter of Dr George Sigerson. Artist and poet. Deeply affected by the executions that followed the 1916 Rising. Died in England. Works include *Collected Poems; The Sad Years*, etc. Poem: *Ireland* 157

GEORGE SIGERSON (1836-1925). Born in Strabane, Co. Tyrone. Educated in Cork and Paris. Scientist and writer. Professor of Biology, UCD. Publications: *The Bards of the Gael and Gall; Modern Ireland*, etc. Poem (trs.): *Jesukin* 35

RICHARD STANIHURST (1545-1618). Born in Dublin. Educated at Oxford and Lincoln's Inn. Returned to Ireland with his Oxford tutor, Edmund Campion, who was later martyred at Tyburn. Contributed to Holinshed's *Chronicles*. After his wife's death he went to Holland and became a priest. Said to be the first important Irish writer to write in English. Died in Brussels. Poem: *A Prayer to the Trinitie* 56

JAMES STEPHENS (1882-1950). Born in Dublin. Self-educated. Lived for a time in Paris and London. Poet, playwright, prose-writer. *The Crock of Gold* is his best-known work. *The Hill of Visions* and *Insurrections* are collections of his poems. Popular broadcaster and debater. Poems: *Donnybrook* 188; *Christmas at Freelands* 188

JOHN STRACHAN (1862-1907). Born in Banffshire, Scotland. Eminent Celtic scholar. With Kuno Meyer he founded the Summer School of Irish Learning in Dublin, 1903. Author of several works on Celtic philology and literature. Poem (trs.): *Prayer to the Virgin* 41

JONATHAN SWIFT (1667-1745). Born in Dublin. Educated at Kilkenny Grammar School and TCD. Dean of St Patrick's Cathedral, Dublin. Remembered for his scathing social and political satires: *Gulliver's Travels; Drapier's Letters; A Modest Proposal*, etc. Less well-known is his practical interest in Dublin's poor, and his founding of St Patrick's Hospital for the insane, the first of its kind in Ireland. Poem: *On a Curate's Complaint of Hard Duty* 72

NAHUM TATE (1652-1715). Born in Dublin. Educated at TCD. Settled in London and wrote plays and poetry. Friend and collaborator of Dryden. His hymns *While Shepherds Watch* and *Through all the Changing Scenes of Life* are still popular. Succeeded Shadwell as Poet Laureate in 1692. Poems: *While Shepherds watched Their Flocks* 69; *As pants the Hart* 70; *Lord, have Mercy* 70

RICHARD CHENEVIX TRENCH (1807-1886). Born in Dublin. Educated at Harrow and Cambridge. Dean of Westminster, and later Archbishop of Dublin. Author of works on history, literature, divinity, philology. Originated the scheme of the Oxford English Dictionary. Works include *Sacred Latin Poetry* and *Poems*. Poem: *Sonnet* 105

KATHERINE TYNAN (1861-1931). Born in Dublin. Educated at Sienna Convent, Drogheda. Began writing poetry at seventeen. Published more than a hundred volumes of prose and verse. Married H. A. Hinkson, writer and lawyer. Died in England. Poems: *Mater Dei* 143; *The Man of the House* 143; *The Making of Birds* 145; *Sheep and Lambs* 146; *Holy Family* 146

HELEN WADDELL (1889-1965). Born in Japan, daughter of an Irish Presbyterian missionary. Educated at the Queen's University, Belfast. Latin scholar and historian. Writings include *Mediaeval Lyrics, The Wandering Scholars*, and *Peter Abelard*, a novel. Poem (trs.): *A Sequence for Saint Michael* 34

LUKE WADDING (died 1657). Born in Dublin. Became a Franciscan friar. Appointed President of the Irish College, Salamanca. Went to Rome in 1618 to promote the Dogma of the Immaculate Conception of the Virgin Mary. Founded Irish College of St Isidore. Died in Brussels. Poem: *Christmas Day is come* 59

LUKE WADDINGE (1600-1691). Born in Wexford of Anglo-Norman stock. Educated in Paris. Succeeded his cousin Bishop French as bishop of Ferns 1684. In that year he published in Ghent *A Small Garland of Pious and Godly Songs Compiled by Luke Wadden, Bishop of Ferns, For the Solace of his Friends and Neighbours in their affliction. The Sweet and the Sour; The Nettle and the Flower; The Thorn and the Rose; Their Garland Compose.* These Christmas carols became popular in Co. Wexford and created a tradition of carol singing which continues today. Poems: *For Christmas Day* 65; *For Saint Stephen's Day* 65; *For Saint John's Day* 66; *For Innocents' Day* 67; *For Twelfth Day* 67

LADY WILDE, SPERANZA (1820-1896). Born Jane Francesca Elgee in Waterford. Married Sir William Wilde, a noted surgeon and President of the Irish Academy. Oscar, their son, is better known than either of them. Lady

Wilde contributed poems to *The Nation* under the pen-name Speranza. She died in poverty in London. Poem: *The Famine Year* 127

OSCAR WILDE (1854-1900). Born in Dublin. Educated at TCD and Magdalen College, Oxford. Achieved fame as a playwright and notoriety for his studied unconventionality. His plays — *Lady Windermere's Fan, The Importance of being Earnest*, etc. — were, and continue to be, most popular. His involvement with Lord Alfred Douglas led to court proceedings which resulted in Wilde's imprisonment for two years. On his release he published *The Ballad of Reading Gaol*. He died in poverty in Paris. Prose works include *The Picture of Dorian Gray* and *De Profundis*, his 'apologia'. Poems: From *The Ballad of Reading Gaol* 139; *E Tenebris* 141; *San Miniato* 142; *Helas!* 142

ROBERT WYSE JACKSON (1908-1976). Educated at Bishop Foy School, Waterford, TCD, Middle Temple and Egerton Hall, Manchester. Bishop of Limerick, Ardfert and Aghadoe 1961-1970. Freeman of Limerick. Publications include *Swift and His Circle* and *King of the Friday*. Poem (trs.): *The Festival of the Nativity* 53

WILLIAM BUTLER YEATS (1865-1939). Born in Dublin. Educated at the High School and Dublin School of Art. Co-Founder of the Abbey Theatre. Regarded as Ireland's greatest modern poet. Awarded Nobel Prize in 1923. Died in France, but is buried in Drumcliffe churchyard, Co. Sligo. Poems: *Sailing to Byzantium* 153; *The Ballad of Father Gilligan* 154; *A Prayer for My Son* 155

INDEX OF POEM TITLES

INDEX OF THEMES

ACKNOWLEDGMENTS

For permission to reprint the poems, acknowledgment is made to the following:

For CHRISTY BROWN: 'Good Friday' from *Background Music*, to Martin Secker and Warburg Limited and to the Estate of Mr Christy Brown, and to Stein and Day Publishers, New York.

For PADRAIG de BRUN: 'Calvary' and 'Is it not You, Lord!' from *Miserere*, to Mrs Maire Cruise O'Brien.

For JAMES BURKE: 'Missionary Hymn', to the Holy Ghost Fathers.

For JOSEPH CAMPBELL: to Mr Simon Campbell.

For VINCENT CAPRANI: 'The Prizefighter's Prayer', from *Rowdy Rhymes and Rec-im-itations*, to the author.

For JAMES CARNEY: 'The Questions of Eithne Alba' from *Medieval Lyrics*, to the author and to The Dolmen Press.

For AUSTIN CLARKE: 'Martha Blake' from *Later Poems* and 'Pilgrimage' from *Pilgrimage and Other Poems*, to Mr Dardis Clarke.

For PADRAIC COLUM: 'Fuschia Hedges in Connacht' from *A Gaelic Anthology* edited by Grace Rhys, and 'An Old Woman of the Roads' and 'A Cradle Song' from *Poets Circuits* to the Estate of Padraic Colum, to Oxford University Press and to The Devin-Adair Co. Inc., Old Greenwich.

For MAURICE CRAIG: 'Ballad to a Traditional Refrain' from *Contemporary Irish Poets* edited by Robert Greacen and Valentine Iremonger (Faber and Faber Limited, Lndon 1949), to the author.

For CYRIL CUSACK: 'Cross Talk' and 'Summer Reflection', to the author.

For CECIL DAY LEWIS: 'Offertorium' from *Requiem for the Living* and 'The Christmas Rose' from *The Gate*, to The Estate of C. Day Lewis and to A.D. Peters and Company Limited.

For JOHN F. DEANE: 'Contact' and 'Offertory' from *Stalking the Time*, to the author and to Profile Press.

For 'LYNN DOYLE': 'An Ulsterman' from *Ballygullion Ballads*, to Mrs Wyn Fisher.

For ROBERT FARREN: 'Stable Straw', 'Lineage', 'Immolation' and 'Sleep' from *Selected Poems*, to the author and to Sheed and Ward Limited.

For ROBIN FLOWER: to Mr Patrick Flower.

For ALICE FURLONG: to The Estate of Alice Furlong.

For THOMAS KINSELLA: 'Exodus to Connacht' and 'A Poem to the Heart of Jesus' from *An Dunaire* and 'Carol' from *Downstream*, to the author and to The Dolmen Press.

For SIR SHANE LESLIE: 'Holy Cross', 'Forest Song', and 'Saint Patrick' from *Verses in Peace and War*, to Burns and Oates Limited.

For WINIFRED M. LETTS: 'Boys', 'Irish Skies' and 'The Harbour' from *Songs from Leinster*, to The Dundalgan Press (W. Tempest) Limited.

For C. S. LEWIS: 'Evensong', 'Prayer' and 'Love's as Warm as Tears' from *Poems*, to Collins Publishers Limited and to Harcourt Brace Jovanovich, New York.

For THE EARL OF LONGFORD: 'Morning Prayer' from *The Dove in the Castle*, to the estate of the author.

For DONAGH MacDONAGH: 'Ballade' from *A Warning to Conquerors*, to Mrs Iseult McGuinness and The Dolmen Press.

For ROY McFADDEN: 'March' from *Selected Poems*, to the author and to The Blackstaff Press.

For LOUIS MacNEICE: 'Prayer before Birth' from *Collected Poems*, and 'A Week to Christmas' from *Autumn Journal*, to Faber and Faber Limited.

For TOMAS MAC SIOMOIN: 'The Silence', a translation of 'An Tost', from *Damhna*, to Sairseal O Marcaigh and to the author.

For JOHN MONTAGUE: 'The Little Flower's Disciple' from *The Leaping Fire* and 'The Answer' from *Chosen Light*, to the author and to The Dolmen Press.

For RAYMOND MURRAY: to the author.

For EOIN NEESON: 'A Prayer for Forgiveness' from *Poems from the Irish*, to the author.

For CATHAL O'BYRNE: 'Christmas Wayfarers' and 'A Donegal Hush Song' from *The Lane of the Thrushes*, to Mr Roland E. Benner.

For FRANK O'CONNOR: 'The Praise of Fionn' and 'The Sweetness of Nature' from *Kings, Lords and Commons*, copyright 1959 by Frank O'Connor, to A.D. Peters and Company Limited and to Joan Daves.

For Fr PATRICK O'CONNOR: 'My Prayer', 'The Lights of Dublin' and 'Exiles' from *Songs of Youth*, to St Columban's Missionary Society and to the author.

For ULICK O CONNOR: 'Repentance' from *Life Styles*, to the translator and The Dolmen Press.

For MAIRTIN O DIREAIN: 'Trees in a Frosty Night' and 'Invitation to Mary' from *Danta*, 1939-1979, to the author and to An Clocomhar Teoranta.

For SEAN O'FAOLAIN: 'At Saint Patrick's Purgatory' from *The Silver Branch*, to the author.

For CHRISTOIR O'FLYNN: 'God?' and 'Sainthood' from *Banana*, to the author.

For BRIAN O'HIGGINS: 'The Mountain Altar' from *Songs of Glen na Mona*, to Mrs Freda O'Higgins.

For MOIRA O'NEILL: 'Grace for Light' from *Songs of the Glens of Antrim*, to William Blackwood and Sons Limited.

For SEAN O RIORDAIN: 'My Mother's Burying' from *Irish Writing* 33 to the estate of Sean O Riordain and to Mr Valentine Iremonger; for 'Freedom', to the estate of Sean O Riordain and to the Reverend C. S. C. Quin.

For COSLETT QUIN: 'Fair is my Lord's Own City' and 'Freedom', to the translator.

For GEORGE RUSSELL: 'Immortality', 'Prayer' and 'Desire', from *Collected Poems*, to Colin Smythe Limited and the A.E. Estate.

For GEORGE SEAVER: 'Communion Hymn', from *Church Hymnal*, to the estate of George Seaver.

For JOHN D. SHERIDAN: 'Joe's No Saint', 'The Priestin' of Father John' and 'To the New Ordained' from *Joe's No Saint*, to Dr J. P. Sheridan.

For JAMES STEPHENS:'Donnybrook', copyright 1915 by Macmillan Publishing Company, renewed 1943 by James Stephens, and 'Christmas at Freelands', copyright 1925, 1926 by Macmillan Publishing Company, renewed 1953, 1954 by James Stephens, to The Society of Authors on behalf of the copyright owner, Mrs Iris Wise, and to Macmillan Publishing Company, New York.

For HELEN WADDELL: 'A Sequence for Saint Michael' from *Medieval Latin Lyrics*, to The Executors of the Estate of Helen Waddell.

For WILLIAM BUTLER YEATS: 'Sailing to Byzantium', 'The Ballad of Father Gilligan', 'A Prayer for My Son' from *The Collected Poems of W. B. Yeats*, to Michael B. Yeats, Anne Yeats and Macmillan London Limited.

For MONK GIBBON: 'French Peasants' and 'The Prayer of the Arab Physician' from *The Velvet Bow*, and 'The Poetry of Gerard Manley Hopkins' from *Seventeen Sonnets*, to the author.

For COTHRAI GOGAN: 'Prayer of a Pagan Woman' and 'Mountain Drive' from *Poems of Prayer*, to the author.

For OLIVER ST JOHN GOGARTY: 'The Airman's Breastplate' from *Collected Poems*, to Mr Oliver D. Gogarty, SC, and to The Devin-Adair Co. Inc., Old Greenwich.

For STEPHEN LUCIUS GWYNN: 'On One dying in a Convent' from *Aftermath* (The Dundalgan Press), to the late Aubrey Gwynn, SJ.

For SEAMUS HEANEY: 'Song of the Soul', to the author; 'Saint Francis and the Birds' and 'Poor Women in a City Church' from *Death of a Naturalist* (Faber and Faber Limited), to the publishers.

ACKNOWLEDGMENTS

For JOHN HEWITT: 'Rome, Sunday June 1960' from *The Rain Dance*, and 'Whit Monday' from *Collected Poems*, to the author and to The Blackstaff Press.

For ELEANOR HULL: 'The Song of Childbirth', 'A Prayer', 'I lie down with God', 'The Soul's Desire' and 'Hymn to the Virgin Mary', from *The Poem Book of the Gael*, to The Editor's Literary Estate and to Chatto and Windus Limited.

For DOUGLAS HYDE: to Mr Douglas Sealy.

For JOHN IRVINE: 'Saint Colm-cille and the Cairn of Farewell', 'Invocation to Saint Bride', 'The little Pets of Saint Mochua' and 'Saint Fiacre', from *A Treasure of Irish Saints*, to Mrs E. McCormack and to The Dolmen Press.

For ROBERT WYSE JACKSON: 'The Festival of the Nativity' from *The Celtic Cross*, to Mrs Lois Wyse Jackson.

For JOHN JORDAN: 'Lolek' from *Celebration*, to the author.

For PATRICK KAVANAGH: 'Advent', 'Canal Bank Walk', 'The One,' 'Ploughman' and 'I may reap' from *Collected Poems*, to Mrs Katherine Kavanagh.

For JOAN KEEFE: 'An Answer to Thomas Barry' from *Irish Poems from Cromwell to the Famine*, to the author and to Bucknell University Press.

For BRENDAN KENNELLY: 'Christ's Bounty', 'Saint, Bird and Angel', 'Jesus on the Sabbath' and 'God's Promises' from *A Drinking Cup;* 'The Pilgrim' from *The Boats are in;* and 'On the Flightiness of Thought', to Professor Brendan Kennelly, to Allen Figgis and Company Limited and to The Gallery Press.